The Mind of the Universe

Dr. Michael H. Likey D.D. Ph.D. PsyThD. H.Dip.

Copyright © 2017 Michael Likey

All rights reserved.

ISBN: 1545463816
ISBN-13: 978-1545463819

DEDICATION

This book is dedicated to my clients, patients, and students past, present, and future. This is also dedicated to my parents, and to my wonderful wife, Susan.

CONTENTS

	Acknowledgments	i
	Introduction	2
1	The Mind of the Universe	5
2	Eastern and Western Psychology	13
3	Self-Hypnosis and Meditation	23
4	Scientific/Affirmative-Prayer	69
5	Prayer Treatments	74
6	Change of Consciousness	80
7	The Four Considerations	82
8	Accessing the Mind of the Universe	85
9	The Universal Mind and Your Health	87
10	In Summation	90
	Conclusion	92
	About the Author	96

ACKNOWLEDGMENTS

My deep appreciation and gratitude goes to everyone in my beloved Winnipeg, Manitoba that I personally knew, know, and met, for their continued inspiration and encouragement; Montreal, next to New York, the greatest city on earth, for being my place of origin, shaping the person I am today; Toronto, and the people I met and personally knew when I was living there, for opening my mind; finally, Vancouver, for opening up my heart about spirituality, and just opening up my eyes in general; my parents, whose unconditional love and support have been unparalleled; finally, to my wife Susan, for her unconditional love, support, and patience.

My further gratitude and appreciation goes to all of you, the real Magic Mike Likey fans, who after thirty-four years, still remember and support me.

Nothing's forgotten. Nothing is ever forgotten.

DISCLAIMER

Advice and instruction on alternative-wellness techniques herein such as hypnosis, meditation, scientific-prayer, etc. as well as lifestyle suggestions, vitamin intake, etc. are for explanation purposes only and are not substitutes for, nor should be mistaken for conventional medicine.

Always seek first the guidance of your healthcare professional before endeavoring to add complimentary medicine/alternative-wellness to your conventional healthcare regiment.

DR. MICHAEL H. LIKEY

INTRODUCTION

"The Mind of the Universe" can be substituted for "The Mind of God", "First Cause", "Universal Intelligence", "Higher Intelligence", Peace, Love, Joy, Wisdom, Creativity, Light, "Higher Thought", "Infinite Intelligence", (used by Napoleon Hill) "Universal Mind", or even God.

Many of the aforementioned are "New Thought"/metaphysical (as opposed to "New Age") terms, all used previously by such luminaries as Ernest Holmes, (the founder of Religious Science/The Science of Mind) P.P. Quimby, (the "father" of New Thought) Mary Baker Eddy, (the founder of Christian Science) and Charles and Myrtle Fillmore. (the founders of Unity Church) I highly recommend you "Google" these names to learn their historical place in New Thought/metaphysical churches, but suffice it to say that all New Thought/metaphysical churches (including my own) preach Higher Intelligence (or The Mind of God/The Mind of the Universe) being omnipotent, omnipresent and omniscient, with the use of "Scientific Prayer"/"Affirmative Prayer"/"Prayer Treatments" and Contact/Mystical/Higher Consciousness Meditation being the foundations of this spiritual movement for self-healing and the healing of others. Refer to any of my twenty-one other texts on these subjects, a list of most of them being at the end of this one.

Another crucial point at this time: there is absolutely no connection between these aforementioned spiritual movements and "Scientology", a completely different faith, although such New Thought/metaphysical terms as "Christian Scientist", and "Soul Scientist" might easily be confused with "Scientology". In fact, New Thought/metaphysics (which includes Unity, Religious Science, Science of Mind, and Christian Science, but NOT Scientology!) have their basis in thousand-year-old far eastern oriental faiths and philosophies including Buddhism, Hinduism, Taoism, along with the teachings of Confucius, Lao Tzu, and Plato. Far eastern practices such as meditation, eastern and western self-hypnosis, as well as Ayurvedic practices and Traditional Chinese Medicine may all be included/comprise New Thought/metaphysics, as opposed to Scientology, which was invented by L. Ron Hubbard, a science fiction writer, in the 20th century! Therefore the basis of New Thought/metaphysics has a very ancient tradition, and is often referred-to as "New Thought Ancient Wisdom", sometimes "New Thought Timeless Wisdom", especially by the New Thought minister Michael Bernard Beckwith, founder of the Agape New Thought ministry.

Having gotten all of this out of the way, I find it ironic that I'm finally tackling the subject of this book, which is essentially God ("Mother/Father God" if you prefer) since everything I do, both professionally and personally, is for service to God! Certainly not the "God" of any man-made religion, or "God" with any religious connotations, but the "God" which is the invisible and creative force that is within us and all things, silently at work continuously in the physical proof of so-called miracles such as the perfect rotation of the planets around the sun; the beauty of nature, the sweet smell of a flower or freshly-cut grass, and all the beasts that inhabit this physical existence; present in the glowing light emanating from the sparkle in one's eyes, or even in a smile; the day-to-day gratitude that we feel for even the smallest of things including our health and our mental faculties and senses; present in the rainbow, the raindrop, or even a tear; present as well in the peace and the joy that we feel; present in a well-executed work of art or music or architecture; present in the compassionate act of gratitude and giving by one person to another. Another term for all of this, I suppose, is Intelligent Design, of which I am, obviously, a great proponent of, after many years of clinical studies of varying groups of meditators and their psychological and spiritual natures, and the resulting papers/reports/books I have written on all of this.

The cynic (or realist) may remind one of the atrocities of the world, or the human injustices that exist, "How and where then, is God in all of these?" he/she may ask. "Why does God allow these things to exist?" the cynic may ponder. Well, even within these so-called non-Godly thoughts, and the aforementioned atrocities, God exists at the very center of all of it, for God, or the Universal Mind, or First Cause is still the controlling Power, for without this creative, non-partisan force, neither the bad nor the good may exist! It is the long-pondered "balance" of light and dark, philosophized in the Tao and its "Yin and Yang"! One cannot exist without the other, each defining the other; the shadow cannot be seen without the light, and conversely the light is invisible without its defining shadows, as in paintings and art; as in music, one cannot simply have all high's nor low's; the playwright would be foolish to write only of a protagonist that was positive, with no conflict, nor evil character for them to define themselves/play off of to clarify who they all are. Good and bad (which is subjective anyway) exists within this physical incarnation, I believe, so that God can make It's Self known, hence the New Thought term, "We are individualized expressions of God", so that God may express through us, as us: the artist, the musician, the transgendered, the beggar, the thief, the bird, the tree. It is this wonder of contrasts which is the creation of the Universal Mind of God, and to find that beauty and sacredness even in the most difficult situation is one of our Soul's Purposes, or the will of God.

This, then, is what the true subject of this book will be: the wonder and beauty, nay the miracles of creation, of the Universal Mind.

1 THE MIND OF THE UNIVERSE

The very title of this chapter (also this book's title) in itself is intriguing, especially if you have little to no experience with New Thought/metaphysics. Recently someone posted on my Facebook feed after a promotional blurb for this book, "Interested." He has completed (like myself) his Doctorate with the University of Sedona/University of Metaphysics and is currently working on his Doctor of Theocentric Psychology, which I completed a few years ago. I found it interesting that he was interested.

To get non-students of New Thought/metaphysics up to speed, I am going to quote from the article on New Thought from Wikipedia:

The **New Thought movement** (also "Higher Thought" is a philosophical movement which developed in the **United States** in the 19th century, considered by many to have been derived from the unpublished writings of **Phineas Quimby**. There are numerous **smaller groups**, most of which are incorporated in the **International New Thought Alliance**.

New Thought holds that *Infinite Intelligence*, or **God**, is **everywhere**, spirit is the totality of real things, true human selfhood is divine, divine thought is a force for good, sickness originates in the **mind**, and "right thinking" has a healing effect.

Although New Thought is neither **monolithic** nor **doctrinaire**, in general, modern-day adherents of New Thought share some core beliefs:

- God or Infinite Intelligence is "supreme, universal, and everlasting";
- **divinity** dwells within each person, that all people are spiritual beings;
- "the highest spiritual principle [is] loving one another unconditionally... and teaching and healing one another"; and

- "our mental states are carried forward into manifestation and become our experience in daily living".

The New Thought movement originated in the early 19th century, and survives to the current day in the form of a loosely allied group of **religious denominations**, authors, **philosophers**, and individuals who share a set of beliefs concerning **metaphysics, positive thinking,** the **law of attraction, healing, life force, creative visualization,** and **personal power**.[6]

The teachings of **Christian Science** are in some ways similar to Quimby's teachings. Its founder, **Mary Baker Eddy**, was a student and patient of Quimby's but she later disavowed his influence on her Christian Science.

This is New Thought/metaphysics in a nutshell, so-to-speak. Instead of the word "God" which is often used, the terms "The Mind of the Universe" can be substituted, as well as "The Mind of God", "First Cause", "Universal Intelligence", "Higher Intelligence", Peace, Love, Joy, Wisdom, Creativity, Light, "Higher Thought", "Infinite Intelligence", (used by author Napoleon Hill of "Think and Grow Rich" fame) and "Universal Mind", as stated earlier. I'm sure that I've forgotten other derivatives, but you get the idea. Why, as both a student of, and practitioner of New Thought/metaphysics I find the term "The Mind of God", or "The Mind of the Universe" particularly empowering, is because by the very nature of it, we possess that Mind within ourselves, and (according to New Thought philosophies) we exist within that very Mind. We are, in essence, a microcosm of the macrocosm: we possess within us, the very same universe that we exist within, or that which is around us! Can you imagine if we harnessed that Power, or realized It, or better yet, Identified with it? Assuming one believes in prayer, would it not be to our advantage to pray from the Mind of God/Mind of the Universe? Then we would know exactly what to pray for, and we would be guaranteed that our prayers would come true! This is following the idea, as well, that God knows what we have need of even before we do! Even the concept of "Soul's Purpose" (which is God's Will for us in this lifetime) is guaranteed that we can potentially live, providing that we heed our Intuition! (or God-Guidance) Therefore, by listening to our Intuition and subsequently following it, we can potentially begin to live a happier, more joy-filled life, filled with true prosperity (not necessarily abundance financially) and perhaps even being guided to be at the right place at the right time to meet our "soul-mate"!

Well and Fine

This is all well and fine, but how does one even begin to hear, or be guided by one's Intuition? How does one harness the Power and Wisdom of God? Moreover, if one is unwell, how do we allow God's Healing Love to take us over and heal us?

As stated earlier, one of the principle spiritual technologies of New Thought/metaphysics is Contact/Mystical/Higher Consciousness Meditation, its purpose being Divine contact, or oneness with the Universal Mind, hence the title "Mystical" Meditation, the search for contact with the Divine being the principle activity of the mystic.

Just imagine: In the beginning there was nothing, then from the nothingness there came Light/First Cause, or God, the Creator who began to create everything so that God could manifest and express through these things in the illusion of the physical form; hence, the illusion of separateness, or individuality, male, female, animal, tree, insect, etc., etc. so that we may do true service, or allow God to create through us! Really, everything started (and still does begin) in the Mind of God/Mind of the Universe as an energetic idea, or frequency, and then begins to take on physical embodiment, shape, and form, or at least the physical illusion of it in the Mind of the Universe, and therefore correspondingly within the world that we are supposedly experiencing with our five (or more) senses. Pretty heady stuff, huh? So if we actually make contact with this Mind of the Universe, and Its frequencies (Love, Peace, Wholeness, etc.) how can we go wrong? Theoretically, as we merge with the Mind of God (consciously or not) and become one with God's healing energies, our Intuition (or God-Guidance) also begins to multiply: we become more Intuitive, or God-Guided as we heal!

The vehicle for all of this is Contact/Mystical Meditation. If we meditate daily for at least twenty minutes, over time we will become increasingly more Intuitive, as well as become healthier mind, body, and soul because we are resonating more and more with the Mind of God. We will begin to be guided to what God's Will is for us in this lifetime, which always results in contentment and happiness. In fact, this is how you know you've made contact with the Mind of the Universe/God: there is a profound relaxation, and feeling of contentment and peace. Another New Thought/metaphysics term, at this point if you will, is Christ-Consciousness, or Christ-Conscious Awareness, which in a nutshell is that point of contact when your soul has become one with the Mind and Spirit of God; you can substitute "Buddha Consciousness", or whatever, but the Christian influence in early New Thought is still evident in this term.

Because meditation is something so important in your everyday routine, I've written many books about it; almost every single one of my other twenty-one books describes either in detail or generally, how to meditate. Here then, is an excerpt from "Mystical Wisdom" about meditation.

Mystical, or Contact Meditation is the basis for your true spiritual evolution and your spiritual practice. Even if you did nothing else but meditate in the way I'm about to describe, you will lead a healthier, prosperous, peaceful, and more fulfilled life. Add a Prayer Treatment or Scientific/Affirmative-Prayer into your practice, and you will truly be on your way to cozying yourself up to God, cleaning up the trash-bin of the various levels of your mind in the process!

Quite simply, Mystical or Contact Meditation attunes you to God's healing energy which is pure Universal love. The more you meditate, the more attuned (and healed) you become!

Keep in mind that what I'm about to describe is not western meditation (consisting of guided meditation designed to temporarily make you feel happy, and/or to eliminate unwanted behaviors (such as over-eating and smoking) as with hypnotherapy, but eastern meditation, designed to be practiced in silence (without someone else speaking/leading you into altered-state) for divine-contact! Hence the name, Contact, or Mystical Meditation. Remember, too, that you must unfailingly practice meditation several times daily, ad infinitum. The length of time with each session will increase, but minimum five minutes at first will be somewhat effective; although your goal will be five minutes, I suspect that you'll go longer, as is the case with most people.

Developing good habits at first is also recommended, such as picking a place in your home that "feels right" for your meditative sessions; sit on a pillow on the floor; sit on your favorite chair; be comfortable above all, as you don't want to be distracted by body discomfort, in fact, you don't want to (and won't) have an awareness of your physical body at all, in time. You can strike a Yoga-pose if it feels right, as long as you can sit for a potentially long time without falling over or falling asleep. Falling asleep is counterproductive, as you want to keep an awareness of your breath (at the very least) let alone of any light and other sensations you might experience, such as joy! Burn any kind of gentle and pleasant-smelling incense if you want, to set a mood; have white candles burning as well if you so desire, both for the mood-setting aspect, as well as the energy-cleansing effects that white candles will have on your environment. Sitting with your back straight will help the twin, serpentine (male/female) Kundalini ("coiled one" in Sanskrit) energies to rise up your spine as they wind their way around it, originating from the base of your spine. The theory is, the base of your spine, like the mercury in a thermometer heats up the longer that you sit, and begins to rise up, carrying the twin energies upward and around your spine. This is an ancient Sanskrit concept that original Primal (God) Energy ("Shakti") exists at the base of the spine, and as it is "awakened" and rises, so that potentially, enlightenment may be achieved. Nonetheless, sitting with your back straight may assist in this occurring, and it will certainly help in keeping you awake!

Next, you must, with eyes gently shut, gaze upward and back, towards your brow, or third-eye area. The third eye (also known as the inner eye) is a mystical and esoteric concept referring to a speculative invisible eye which provides perception beyond ordinary sight. In certain dharmic spiritual traditions such as Hinduism, the third eye refers to the ajna, or brow, chakra. It has been clinically proven that if you gaze upward and back (with eyes open or shut) towards your brow-area, a strain will be created on your eyes, thus resulting in you closing your eyes and going into an altered-state naturally. As a clinical hypnotherapist, I have used this method many times! After about a minute or so, the subject always seems to "drift off", so-to-speak. As with hypnosis, focusing on something, as well as repetition, is important at this point while meditating: follow the rhythm of your breath while gazing upon your brow, or third-eye area. Be aware of the in-breath, the out-breath, and then back to the in-breath again as never-ending occurrences. In lieu of the in-and-out focusing, you can, as in Zen, focus instead on the up and downward movement of your breath: on the in-breath the "up", on the out-breath, the "down"; in time you can follow this as a never-ending cycle, or ball. Choose which feels right. Now, for health purposes you must also add this: (as in Traditional Chinese Medicine it is believed that the "chi" is the life-force, originating in the belly, or "dantien") on the "in-breath", your tummy expands to take in the chi, and on the "out-breath", the tummy will contract, releasing the chi, again, in a never-ending cycle. This is in lieu of you using your lungs (which is the opposite: expanding on the inhale and contracting on the exhale) Using your dantien in this way supposedly adds years to your life.

It really is not so much to think about, and in no time you will be doing all of this at once! Remember: eyes closed, third-eye-gazing, focusing on your breath while tummy expands and contracts. That's all you need to do initially. Practice this for months, lengthening your meditation sessions to twenty-minutes. Twenty-minutes is all you really need, but if you can go longer, all the better!

In time, you may begin to see a light at your brow, or third-eye area. This is good. If not, begin to visualize light emanating from both your third-eye and heart-chakra area. They need not be any specific colors, but if you want to, imagine one gold, the other one, white. Imagine the light from your heart (soul) chakra pulsating towards and into your head, to encourage that Intuition, or God-Guidance! That's it! If you can meditate like this for twenty-minutes (at least) twice-a-day, you are well on your way to better health, peace, and prosperity!

I would be at fault at this point if I were not to mention what Dr. Masters refers to as the "Outer-Closure" techniques from his "Meditation Dynamics" course.   These were also some of the techniques given to me by a mahatma when I was twenty-nine. The idea being, is that you are shutting out any exterior and environmental sights and sounds so that you can completely focus (and welcome the experiences) of the divine.

In the first technique, or 'Light', the meditator focuses on their forehead, at a spot between, and a little above the eyebrows. The thumb and first two fingers of the dominant hand help with this, the index finger resting lightly on the correct spot on the forehead, and the thumb and middle finger resting lightly on each closed eyeball, to steady and stop the eyeballs from moving. Where you are to actually focus your sight is never stated - do you stare through the colored shapes and blackness behind the closed eyelids into infinity ? Do you focus right on the back of your eyelids, trying to make sense of the swirling colors, the 'black light', you see there ? Do you actually focus not on what you see, but on the spot on your forehead where your index finger rests ? Do you turn your eyeballs upwards to this spot, or do you keep a level horizontal gaze ?

In the second technique, or 'Music', the meditator stops their ears with each thumb, twisting slightly so that the fingers of each hand rest on the top of the head. The technique is then to listen to what you hear, the Sound of the Spheres, or the sound of silence. Or is it a sound like a waterfall ? Is that just a physical manifestation of the pulse in the thumbs in the ear, or the trapped air in the closed ear canal ? And if it is, do you listen to it, or do you listen through it, trying to find some ineffable celestial sound beyond it ? Are you trying to listen to a silence beyond it ?

These first two techniques involve placing one hand (in the first technique) or both hands (in the second) up to your head. This can be tiring and cause arm muscle fatigue. For the first sixteen or so years that Prem Rawat was teaching in the West, it was common for meditators to use a 'beragon', which was an arm rest shaped like a letter 'T' about 2 feet high - the bottom of the stem of the 'T' rested on the floor or cushion you were sitting on, and each elbow rested on the crosspiece of the T. In the mid-eighties, Prem Rawat discouraged the use of beragons, or any form of arm rest, and the meditator was required to hold their arms up without support. Beragons are recommended by other Gurus and indeed one design has been patented.

The third technique, or 'Holy Name', or 'The Word', is simply to follow your breath. Many meditation traditions involve watching the breath in some way, but most traditions give clear instructions on how to do this, since in fact you can use your breath in many different ways to create many different mind states. Prem Rawat says very little about it. His most common instruction while demonstrating the technique is to move his hand up and down in front of him as he breathes in and out, the implication being that you are to follow the in-breath and out-breath upwards and downwards (or is it downwards and upwards ?) from your nose to the base of the lungs or the abdomen and up again. Another instruction he sometimes gives is that you follow your breath like you are sitting on an inner swing, with Prem Rawat pushing this swing. This is one of the clearest signs in recent times that Rawat is still inferring that he is a power inside the meditator helping and guiding their meditation.

The fourth and final technique, or 'Nectar', involves curling the tongue upwards and placing the tip of the tongue...where ? Well, for many years, the instruction was to place it on the roof of the mouth as far back as you could possibly force it, the goal being to make it go behind the uvula (the little skin flap that hangs down at the throat entrance), and up the rear nasal passage as far as you could. The ultimate fanciful notion was to touch the base of the brain, and make a cosmic connection, although there are no reports of anyone being actually able to do this. Turning the tongue back in this way is a well known yoga technique called *kechari mudra* . In more recent times, Prem Rawat has dropped all reference to the uvula, and just required the meditator to rest the tip of the tongue on the roof of the mouth in a manner that is comfortable, even if they cannot get it any higher than the back of their front teeth. But again, on what is the meditator to focus ? Just where the tip of the tongue is physically, or through it in some sense, or do you focus on what you taste ?

The aforementioned techniques may sound culturally foreign to you, but all have their basis either in Zen Buddhism, and/or Hinduism. The "Nectar" technique, for example, is as old as time, and specific to mystics in Hinduism; the act of putting your tongue as far back while touching the tip to the roof of your mouth also creates a calming physiological effect; in Traditional Chinese Medicine, the roof of the mouth/palate and anus are specific energy-points ("Hui yin" points) where one might lose energy or "chi", therefore by "shutting" them, you develop your chi for better health and longevity!

Practice all or some of the techniques I've shared here, and enjoy doing them, for they are the very crucial basis of your spiritual practice, and the key to oneness with your Higher Self, or God. They are also crucial to your health and wellness mind, body, and soul, as well as being the most important key to prayer.

Now that you are aware of how to meditate, and the importance of a regular and ongoing practice of it for your health and spiritual development, (especially for access and contact with the Mind of the Universe/God) in time you will begin to develop your Intuition, and eventually live your God-Guided Soul's Purpose, for a happier and more prosperous life. Let's move on to Eastern and Western Psychology, so that you can better understand how the human mind works (or doesn't) as opposed to your Higher Mind/Mind of the Universe/Mind of God and how it woks so that you may have a more clinical understanding of the human mind, meditation, and the Mind of God.

2 EASTERN AND WESTERN PSYCHOLOGY

At the risk of repeating myself, I have chosen to quote myself from one of my other books, "Mystical Wisdom Complete". Following this chapter, we will also compare Eastern and Western Self-Hypnosis and Meditation, as a means to access the Higher Mind/Mind of the Universe, again, from a previously-published book of mine.

Metaphysical Psychology and Western Psychology

Very basically, western psychologists define a "neurotic" mind as one that cannot relate to, or adapt to, its exterior environment. When this occurs, the therapist trains and treats the mind to relate to whatever current, exterior environmental situation exits, so that the person being treated does not retreat into a fantasy-world situation created by their mind. Unfortunately for the patient, their environment will inevitably change, evolve, and grow again, upon which time further analysis/psychological treatment will be required again for their adapting to these new changes. Western psychology therefore fails as far as permanent results for the patient are concerned.

Eastern, or "Spiritual/Metaphysical Psychology" provides a permanent solution for the patient, whereby no ongoing, or occasional "upgrading" is required (Illustration 3).

Spiritual Mind-Science and Psychology vs. Traditional Psychology

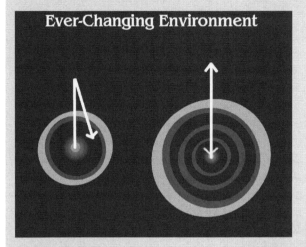

Illustration 3

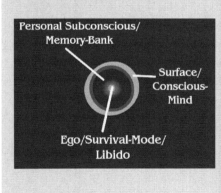

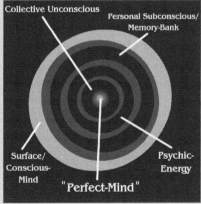

How is this accomplished?

We must delve a little deeper into the nature of western and Metaphysical Psychology to understand this.

Western psychology provides as an "anchor" or basis of the human-mind the "Libido", or "Survivor-Instinct" which apparently (according to western psychology) exists in the "Personal Subconscious"-level of the mind, just beneath the "Conscious"-level of the mind. (Illustrations 4) Within this "Personal Subconscious" mind also exists memories accumulated from events that occurred in the "Conscious" awareness/physical environment of the subject. Both western and Metaphysical Psychologists agree on the existence of the "Conscious" and "Personal Subconscious" (or "Memory-Bank") levels of the mind. Metaphysical, or Spiritual Psychology deviates from western psychology after that.

Metaphysical Psychologists believe that the basis or "anchor" of the human-mind is not the Libido, but God, Perfect-Mind, or Source. Furthermore, several other levels of the mind exist, according to Spiritual/Metaphysical Psychology. (Illustration 5)

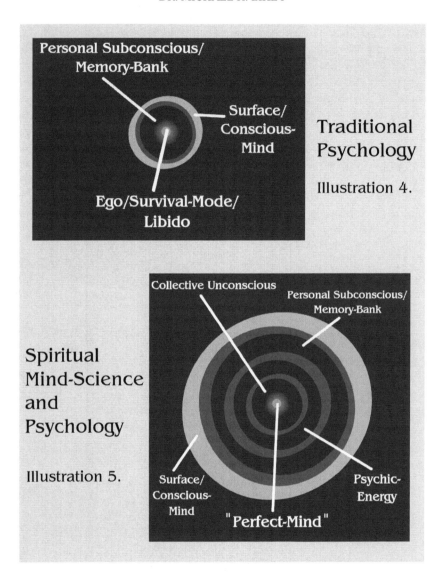

Illustration 4. Traditional Psychology

Illustration 5. Spiritual Mind-Science and Psychology

One level up from the center, or God, or "Perfect Mind" exists what Carl Jung called the "Collective Unconscious", wherein we hold "archetypes" or symbolic-representations of people we have encountered in our environment, or Conscious-level of our mind. Jung referred to these archetypes as the "gods and goddesses" of our mind. More accurately, someone who may have hurt us in the past may be represented unconsciously as a "demon" or "devil", or a "temptress", "shrew", "whore", etc. The patient may therefore see themselves symbolically and unconsciously at that level of their mind as a "victim". Conversely a healthy mind may contain images of the owner of the mind as the "artist", "seeker", "prince", "princess", "Mother Goddess", etc. In theory, from a metaphysical perspective, these unconscious archetypes (or how the patient unconsciously "sees" themselves and others) will cause them to give out a certain "vibe", which will often translate/extend to the physical. How often have we seen people shuffling along, head lowered and shoulders drooped, with very little energy? Often these people are not even consciously aware of their feelings/emotions/visuals of themselves! We might say that "life" has caused them to be "worn down". In extreme cases, this vibration/resonation/unconscious attitude begins to affect the physical health of the person, let alone their emotional well-being. This level of the mind that holds the vibration of the person's archetypes is called the "Psychic-Energy Level", because the person will give out on a "psychic (or non-physical) energy-level a "feeling" or resonation or vibration of how they really see themselves and others unconsciously. This is often why a person who is resonating out anger or bitterness will attract to themselves someone with a similar vibration: either attracting conflict, or friends/partners or "birds of a feather" who "flock together". "Misery loves company". Happiness/positive attitude attracts and perpetuates happier people and situations.

Similarly, when there are two pianos in a room, and a note is struck in one piano, the same string will resonate by itself, and automatically, within the other piano. Try this.

The next levels up from the center are the Personal Subconscious or Memory-Bank, and Conscious-level as previously discussed.

The Metaphysical Psychologist therefore has a chance to work with more levels of a person's mind to help them more completely and permanently resolve the patient's emotional hindrances, with God as the basis, as opposed to the ever-changing physical environment as a basis.

Psycho-Physical Unit

As previously stated, in Metaphysical Science and Psychology, the term "Psycho-Physical Unit" refers to the fact that the mind affects the body (as previously discussed) and the body affects the mind. For example, if you are not feeling physically well, you often are not feeling happy or in a good mood.. (Illustration 6) Which came first? The bad mood which caused the physical issue, or vice-versa?

Spiritual Mind-Science and Psychology: Psycho-Physical Units

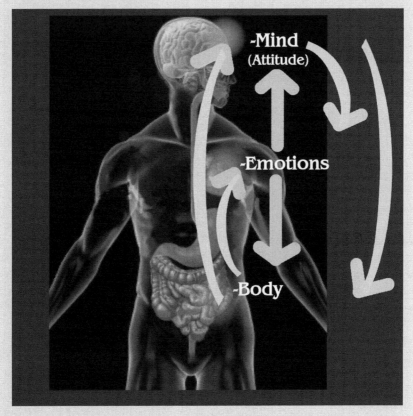

Illustration 6.

This is also another basis of a branch of metaphysics called "New Thought", recently brought to mass consciousness by the DVD "The Secret", but originally observed, documented, and practiced in mid-1800's eastern United States by Phineas Parkhusrt Quimby. (Seale, 1986)
 Quimby was a clockmaker, who used hypnosis (then called "Mesmerism" named after the 18th-century German therapist and practitioner Franz Anton Mesmer) to cure his patients of physical and emotional illnesses. He

did this by "magnetizing" them. The word "magnetizing" at the time was interchangeable with hypnotizing/putting into trance/meditative state of the client or patient. Quimby would then use suggestions similar to what Milton Erickson would later develop as N.L.P. or Neuro-Linguistic Programming, to change the negative thinking of the patient, substituting positive for negative thought-patterns. This was also the forerunner to Clinical Hypnotherapy. If appropriate for the particular patient, (who at the time was often religious) Quimby would quote religious scripture while they were hypnotized/in meditative state to "prove" and "talk the patient out of" negative thinking. This was the forerunner to Ernest Holmes' Religious Science/Science of Mind and Unity. One of Quimby's many successes was a patient whose name was Mary Baker Eddy. Her husband, a medical doctor, took his invalid wife to see Quimby. She was bedridden for many years, but after Quimby cured her, she could walk, spreading and practicing this new therapy/movement that she called New Thought for many years after Quimby's death.

To say that Quimby "cured" his patients would be inaccurate, and Quimby himself would no doubt agree: the patients cured themselves. His use of meditation/mesmerism/hypnosis so that the patients "new thoughts" would impact more greatly on their unconscious mind and therefore affect in positive ways their emotional and physical health is a more accurate description.

One might therefore, in Metaphysical terms, say "the spirit (God) heals the soul, which heals the mind, which heals the body". Quimby used whatever verbage he was guided to use, to convince/argue/explain to the heart and soul of the patient (their mind) of the cause of their illness, helping them see the illogic of it (again, in their mind), which in turn helped them emotionally to feel better immediately with this "knowing", and consequently eliminate the physical symptoms. He said "the reason for the illness is the cure".

In metaphysics it is believed that the mere practice of meditation heals the person, because this practice of "Divine Union"/Mystical Meditation/Divine Contact whether conscious or not, heals the soul which heals the mind which heals the body. We are Psycho-Physical units.

All of this came about because of Quimby's studies, documentation, and practice. Today we recognize in western psychology that meditation/hypnosis makes the mind more susceptible to suggestions, therefore if the therapist logically reasons out the source of the patient's issues, the information will sink deeper into their mind, and be more long-lasting. If the therapist (as in Metaphysical Psychology) heals/changes the patients archetypes within the Collective Unconscious, as well as the traumas within the memory-bank, or Personal Subconscious of their mind, at the same time, under hypnosis/meditation creating a safe and permanent

Higher Authority/situation (God, or the patient's concepts of God, again, permanently fixed in their unconscious mind, and substituted for anything negative via hypnosis/meditation), then this is in Metaphysical Psychology referred to as a Meditational, or Metaphysical/Spiritual Mind-Treatment. Many of the techniques found in western psychology, therefore, have their roots in eastern/spiritual mysticism, including the use of hypnosis, or meditation.

One may see now how the aforementioned western psychological modalities such as N.L.P., Clinical Hypnotherapy, and even Cognitive Therapy (which seeks to help the client overcome difficulties by identifying and changing dysfunctional thinking, behavior, and emotional responses. This involves helping clients developing skills for modifying beliefs, identifying distorted thinking, relating to others in different ways, and changing behaviors) were influenced by these earlier Metaphysicians such as Quimby, Holmes, and even Jung.

Psychosomatics: Complete Misunderstandings

Currently, (early twenty-first century) the term "psychosomatic" generally has negative implications. It suggests that a person's illness is "all in their head", or imagined. This is a misinterpretation of the original use of the word.

In fact, the term originally referred to the fact that a person's illness *originates* in their mind, an accurate diagnosis, since thoughts/beliefs/traumas in the personal subconscious and collective unconscious mind affects the body, emotions, and spirit, as metaphysicians have proven eons ago, and from which starting-point metaphysicians work from to heal their patients. Heal the patient's traumas contained in the various levels of the unconscious human-mind via faith by substituting and anchoring faith/peace/love/joy/Higher Consciousness/God for fear, etc. (as also explained previously) and the physical ailment(s) will disappear, using the tools of scientific/affirmative-prayer and meditation. The term psychosomatics could be used when working with patients as Psycho-Physical Units, as explained earlier. I like to use the term "Spiritual Psychosomatics" when working with people as Psycho-Physical Units, that is to say that the spirit/Higher Consciousness may be accessed from deep within the mind in order to heal the mind which in turn heals the body.

Spiritual Psychosomatics

Refer to Ernest Holmes' book "Living the Science of Mind" (1984, DeVorss & Company, California) if this subject interests you, for he goes into greater detail about this, but never uses the term "Psycho-Physical Units" to describe the mind-body-spirit relationship.

In fact, a slight deviation within Religious Science/Science of Mind is the belief that the spirit is contained within the mind, the spirit and mind therefore being linked; heal the mind (which contains the spirit) and the spirit will work through the body to heal the body via the mind-spirit connection.

Nowadays modern science, quantum science and physics has proven that energy/power/light exists at the very centre of atoms (and now sub-atomic particles!) which is what everything is comprised of. Nobody can see electricity, but we know that it's there, working and materializing as the lighting up of a bulb, for example. Nobody can see gravity, but we know that it's a law at work. All we need do is drop an object and see it fall to the ground. These are invisible things, but they are real and at work constantly. (Byrnes, 2006)

Nobody sees "spirit", or "God", or the "soul, but we know it's there because we have faith that it exists, and we can feel "spirit"/God/our soul as our joy in a sunset, or in the awe we experience when we look out at the stars and planets, or in the feeling we experience as wonder at the marvels of birth, let alone the miracles of everything else around us. This is how "spirit"/God/"Light"/"Love" manifests and proves its existence: the proof is in the existence of those feelings. These feelings are accessed at the very depth of our soul, at the very center of our mind, where we can imagine and create, for creation/creativity/imagination is also defined as God by some. (Holmes, 1998) Since existence/creation is everywhere, there is no place God/light/love/existence is not.

What naturally follows is that everything (including the body and the mind) is comprised of spirit/creation/existence or the "invisible". The spirit may be accessed consciously or not (it doesn't necessarily matter whether or not you are having some sort of conscious experience during meditation), via the route of Higher Consciousness meditation (or "Mystical Meditation") through the mind, and since the spirit runs through the mind and body, affecting them based on our attitudes and outlook, and because of the automatic linking/associating/oneness of mind/body/spirit, the healing powers of creation itself subsequently heals the mind/emotions and physical during the meditation process. (Holmes, 1998)

The Power

What we should also note and expand somewhat on is that this same power that exists at the very centre and nucleus of everything may be compared with in scope to the same power that was unleashed or accessed during the splitting of the atom. (Holmes, 1998)

Imagine this power that we unconsciously access through meditation! There is nothing that cannot be accomplished via this power, and it is at our disposal constantly, existing at the core of everything including our mind! Whether or not the stimulation of the pineal gland in our brain through meditation accomplishes this reaction matters not; faith is not about the "how" but the doing and accepting. Higher Consciousness meditation combined with scientific/affirmative-prayer allows the mind to work with this power to encourage miraculous transformation, or evolving/unfolding of the soul. The use of these specific methodologies (and the specific formula/steps) is why we can call this a "scientific treatment" as the results have already been proven many times over; it is no longer theory, but proven spiritual science fact. (Holmes, 1998)

3 SELF-HYPNOSIS AND MEDITATION

The tools for accessing the Mind of the Universe/God are both clinical and metaphysical/mystical, and therefore gifts from the east as well as the west. This chapter, originally titled "Hypnosis Vs. Meditation" from my book, "Mystical Wisdom Complete" will shed more light on this subject.

Hypnosis Vs. Meditation

The title is a bit of a misnomer; herein we are not going to pit hypnosis against meditation, but rather we will compare the differences and the similarities between the two, so that you can make more informed choices, both as a therapist, and/or a patient, and also for your spiritual practice. You may prefer to practice Self-Hypnosis as opposed to Meditation, or vice-versa, in order to have a mystical experience/divine contact. (hence the name of the book, Mystical Self-Hypnosis) As a therapist, you'll no doubt find (as I have) that some of your clients/patients/students will prefer one over the other for various reasons. This is the whole purpose of this book: for you or others to make informed choices. As well, I'm including a basic primer on the workings of the human brain, in addition to the differences between western and eastern psychology, as well as various New Thought/Metaphysical/Mystical tools and technologies such as Mystical/Contact Meditation and Scientific or Affirmative-Prayer, again as self-help methodologies, as well as for potential tools to add to your existing therapist practice. Let's "dig in", so-to-speak!

Firstly, imagine an office building. Next, imagine that you are taking the elevator up to the twentieth floor of that building. Next, after exiting the elevator, you begin to walk along the length of that floor's corridor. As you gaze to the left of you, you peer inside the door marked "Hypnotherapy"; here is what you see inside: a cozy but modern room, equipped with a desk, an office-chair, filing cabinet, etc. Beside the office chair and slightly to the left is a couch or recliner. This is where the clients/patients lay during a treatment. You glance upward, and on the ceiling is a small red sticker; when the patient looks up at the ceiling and slightly back, they will stare at the red dot over and over again until they get drowsy. Beside the couch or recliner is a small stereo speaker, out of which relaxation music or nature-sounds sometimes emanates. On the doctor's desk is a small pocket-watch and chain, which he sometimes uses as a fixation-point in lieu of the red dot. This he swings gently in front of the patient to lull them into slightly altered-state. As another alternative, there is a small pen-light in his pocket, used also instead of the red dot. This light is gazed upon by the patient, as it is steadily held above their head and slightly back, causing their eyes to get heavy and tire as they gaze upward and back. In front of the couch/recliner and resting upon its own table is an hypnotic-wheel, which when electronically activated, spins 'round and 'round; used as yet another fixation tool, the movements of the concentric spirals will lull the patient into altered-state. This wheel may also be a program on the doctor's laptop, activated as needed. These are only some of the tools, besides his voice, which are used by the hypnotherapist.

You exit that office, and continue to walk along the corridor.

Several doors further down the hallway and to your right is another door left ajar and to your right; on it is marked "Meditation". As you enter into that office, you notice immediately the smell of incense. It's a pleasant, almost sweet or floral scent, which is both welcoming and relaxing. A large bouquet of flowers sits upon a nearby alter, and there are throw-pillows of varying colors everywhere, inviting one to sit on the floor. The sparsely furnished office offers full-color, framed pictures on the walls of a blue Buddha, and various other Hindu-gods, as well as multi-colored lotuses. The dimly-lit room is illuminated by a multitude of white candles, which create dancing shadows upon the walls. There are a couple of tapestries on two of the walls, as well as a bamboo curtain over the doorless entryway into the adjacent room. You can hear the bubbling of a small, bamboo fountain upon a Chinese-style, carved table, as well, there is a small sound-system, out of which New Age relaxation music is emanating; occasionally there will be recordings of nature-sounds coming from the machine. There is also an office-desk and chair, as well as a recliner nearby; adjacent to that is a filing cabinet.

These are the only differences between hypnotherapists and mystics. The furniture, decorations, object, tools, and trappings all relate to the particular genre, and that's where the differences end. Sometimes a hypnotherapist may also be a mystic, and have the luxury of offering his/her clients hypnotherapy (if he/she is qualified to do so) or meditation, as some clients prefer one over the other for various reasons.

Following is what the hypnotherapist and meditation-therapist have in common.

They both must lull the patient into an altered-state, either alpha or theta brainwave-state. Alpha is light, meditative-state which can help the therapist to alter the patient's unwanted behaviors such as smoking or overeating; sometimes past-lives may be accessed at this brainwave-level. Theta is a deeper, near-sleep brainwave-state, where the subject is more susceptible to suggestions given by the therapist, and those suggestions can go deeper into the subconscious mind and take hold. Life-between-lives, or soul regression may be accomplished at this brainwave-state. Besides self-worth and worthiness issues, more mystical issues may be addressed here too, such as divine-contact.

Both therapists use their voice to lull participants into altered/meditative-state; the hypnotherapist may use an hypnotic-wheel, while the mystic may use his/her voice and the smell of incense for focusing and relaxation. The steps to hypnosis are: induction, focusing/concentration, repetition, deepening, suggestions, (relating to self-esteem, stop smoking, or eating less) then awakening. The steps to a Meditative Mind-Treatment/Scientific-Prayer Treatment are while in light, meditative-state: Unifying/Identifying, (same as an induction/focusing/concentration/repetition) denying, affirming/proclaiming, (same as suggestions) releasing, (same as awakening) and stating "And So It Is!" a Neuro Linguistic Programming-like suggestion/declaration which anchors the thought/affirmation into the subconscious mind. Light meditative-state is simply accomplished by focusing (with eyes closed) up into the brow/third-eye area, focusing on the repetitiveness of the inhalation and exhalation of one's breathing, visualizing light at the brow and heart-chakra areas and continuing to follow the breath. It's been clinically proven that looking up and back will lull someone into light, meditative-state within a minute or so.

You can see now the similarities and differences between the techniques of the mystic vs. the hypnotherapist, as well as the different objectives and outlooks of each. The mystic may be more focused on divine-contact, whereas the hypnotherapist may more be focused on altering unwanted behaviors.

Dissertation

Following is my dissertation on Self-Hypnosis Vs. Meditation, written as partial fulfillment for one of my degrees.

Because it is crucial to completely understand the therapeutic and non-therapeutic value of self-hypnosis, hetero-hypnosis, and meditation as we study Mystical Self-Hypnosis, I am including here one of my dissertations concerning this same subject-matter.

Introduction

I find it necessary to write this essay, entitled "Hypnosis or Meditation?" primarily because of my passion for my professional work as a Hypnotherapist, and also because of my passion for teaching Meditation. It is also because I have successfully treated and assisted my clients in re-empowering themselves using either Hypnosis or Meditation, without limiting myself or the patient to one method or the other, that I feel compelled to write this essay, as well.

The areas of Non-Metaphysical (or Clinical) Hypnotherapy I have, and am currently practicing in, include: Weight-Control, Smoker's Therapy (Stop-Smoking), Self-Esteem, Relaxation, and Fear Elimination Therapy. The areas of Metaphysical Hypnotherapy I am currently working in, include Past-Life Regression, Soul (or Life-Between-Lives) Regression, and I have done so for more than ten years. I have seen incredible breakthroughs for my clients and patients as a result of all of these practices. The areas of Meditation I am teaching, currently, are both Western (techniques, including, but not limited to, positive affirmations and visualizations for altering unwanted thoughts, behaviors, and improving health, overall) and Eastern Meditation (for experiencing God-Mind, Higher Consciousness). I was given the Eastern Meditation techniques more than twenty-eight years ago, by an Indian Mystic, or Mahatma ("holy-person") while I was on a journey of personal self-growth. These "keys" for going inward, and the resulting experiences, have been providing clear answers for me on every level of my existence ever since. It is no wonder that I am an enthusiastic advocate and teacher of Meditation!

In addition, I have been teaching both "moving-meditation" (Tai Chi) and "stillness-meditation", (Qi Gong) for ten years. One might categorize Qi Gong as "stillness-meditation", as the practitioner stands, sits or lays in silent contemplation and focuses, while Tai Chi may be called "moving meditation", because the practitioner meditates while performing various graceful movements. The goal of Tai Chi and Qi Gong is not to experience the Divine, according to Wang and Liu (1995), but merely to improve and maintain one's health. It is also because of my professional background and years of experience that I feel qualified to write this essay.

It has been my professional observation over the years, that, "Clinical" Hypnotherapists will often limit their practice to only employing Hypnosis only, while often ignoring and neglecting Meditation, even when qualified and capable of practicing it, for their clients, if that method might better suit the "personality" or receptiveness of that client.

Within the context of this work, I intend to clearly define the terms "Clinical Hypnotherapy", "Meditation", and "Self-Hypnosis", as they will be utilized within this essay.

I intend to also describe the techniques, goals and brainwave-states unique and common to Hypnosis and Meditation, and the specific, unique and common benefits that Meditation and Hypnosis has had on my patients.

In addition, I intend to illustrate how Clinical Hypnotherapists may apply Meditation or Self-Hypnosis for the Metaphysical as well as non-Metaphysical (Clinical) benefit of their patients, as well as how Practitioners of Metaphysics/Meditation Teachers may apply "Clinical" Hypnosis for the Metaphysical and non-Metaphysical (Clinical) benefit of their students and clients. I intend to do this by sharing a number of practical examples from my case-files. Of course, the names and details of my clients have been changed to maintain their anonymity.

It is my hope, that by writing this essay, more Metaphysicians and Clinical Hypnotherapists will successfully treat and assist their clients, students, and patients in re-empowering themselves, by not limiting themselves or their clients, to employing one method over the other.

You decide: "Hypnosis or Meditation?"

Review of Literature

The amount of literature that exists on the topics of Hypnosis and Meditation is endless. So too, are the schools of thought on each of them. Everything from "channeled" information, to the findings of science, clinically analyzing the brainwave-states, and measuring the Meditation and/or Hypnosis experiences.

After graduating from the Robert Shields College some years ago, (I will be referring to information from this course for this thesis) where I earned my Clinical Hypnotherapy degree, in addition to doing much of my own subsequent research which included almost every single hard-copy and online journal regarding Hypnosis for therapeutic purposes, I began to appreciate that online (or "Distant-Learning") school from England that Principal Shields started back in 1986. Robert Shields, himself, started off as a Metaphysician, earning a solid reputation in England, which included many regular television, and newspaper appearances. At the age of forty, (he is well-past retirement age at this writing) Shields entered the more clinical field of Hypnotherapy, where he continued to help others to grow, and to heal. What eventually followed, was a Hypnotherapy school, founded by Shields. This college was to be more than a school that teaches their students how to do a simple Induction, (more on this later) a Deepening, (again, more on this later) eventually resulting in a client who remembers their former traumas. This was, and is, a school that ethically educates the potential therapist in how to safely and effectively use hypnosis for freeing the client of debilitating thoughts and behaviors. I have even learned the necessity of qualifying (or screening) clients, lest permanent emotional damage results in hypnotizing them. Unlike many other schools, (I personally know of a colleague, who upon graduating from a local Hypnotherapy school, now takes on any and all clients) Shields also informs us of what to look for in a client, (through a question-period) which would indicate to us that we should not hypnotize them, nor take them on as Hypnotherapy-clients. (This includes such "contra-indications" as depression, and being on anti-depressants within the last six months, for example) What is included, as well, (I understand that many Hypnotherapy schools do not include these) are small courses on N.L.P., (Neuro-Linguistic Programming) Psychology, Past-Life Regression, Self-Hypnosis, Dream Analysis, and much more, which I have researched, can separately cost thousands and thousands of dollars each. Methods for "Uncovering" (or discovering) the root-causes of unwanted behaviors, in addition to Weight-Loss and Stop-Smoking therapies, make for an intensive, (and exhausting) but comprehensive course. What I have found the most impressive, however, is that Shields has never limited himself, his student nor his clients, to any one specific mode of therapy or treatment, be it metaphysical, or clinical in nature. The client's good health is all that matters. If a Past-Life Regression will free them from a current-life trauma, because they understand, now, where they are coming from as far as their soul's growth is concerned, according to Goldberg (1998) so be it. Or, if it takes numerous sessions of uncovering, year-by-year, a client's activities until the specific trauma which caused their current emotional debilitation is discovered, so be it, whatever it takes. Utilize metaphysical or clinical methodologies, this is one of the many things I got out of my education with Robert Shields, whether this was his conscious intention or not: a balance of the metaphysical, as well as the clinical. Thankfully, both my professional and personal backgrounds include the Metaphysical, as well as the Clinical. I will be referring to Robert Shields College of Hypnotherapy course, (1986) for the Clinical Hypnotherapy techniques contained there in.

Dr. Bruce Goldberg is a Doctor of Dentistry, with a background in

Biology, Chemistry and Counseling Psychology. Yet he is most famous for his Oprah, Donahue, Montel, and Regis television appearances on Past and Future-Life Regressions. He sells countless numbers of books, tapes and CD's on these subjects, which are Metaphysical in nature, and yet his education is nothing less than medical/scientific/clinical in nature. He is a Clinical Hypnotherapist, yet one of his many books, "New Age Hypnosis" (published in 1998) contains "how to" topics such as "receiving spiritual guidance from your higher self or masters", "contact departed loved ones", "contact the souls of unborn babies", and so on. I am sure that Dr. Goldberg knows what sells, but he also knows who he is, what his passions are, and what his clients need. He, too, doesn't limit himself to utilizing Metaphysical or Clinical methodologies, in order to assist his clients. For this reason, I refer to Dr. Goldberg's book, for some definitions, and to cross-reference techniques (both Metaphysical and non-Metaphysical) for the purposes of this thesis.

William W. Hewitt, (deceased) with his background as a professional writer/editor, Clinical Hypnotherapist and professional Astrologer, lectured on such topics as mind power, self-improvement, and Metaphysics. His extensive series of books and tapes were on such seemingly-diverse themes as Psychic Development, Tea-Leaf Reading, Stop Smoking and Weight-Loss. Upon closer inspection of his Hypnosis techniques, one will see a great overlap between Metaphysics and the clinical. It is for this reason, that I make reference, for the purposes of this thesis, to his book "Hypnosis for Beginners" (1997) for both the clinical and metaphysical Hypnotherapy and Self-Hypnosis techniques.

In his nearly-three-hundred-page-book, "The Everything Hypnosis Book", (2003) Michael R. Hathaway spans the spectrum from Meditation, to Clinical and non-Clinical Hypnosis, covering such subjects as the history of Hypnosis, "Instant Hypnosis", "Reasons to Change a Habit", "Improving Your Health", Meditation techniques vs. Hypnotic techniques, and much, much, more. This is an easy-to-read, well-illustrated tome (in the style of those "Idiot's Guide" books) and that's why I liberally refer to it for comparisons and similarities between Meditation and Hypnosis.

Finally, Dr. Paul Leon Masters' "University of Metaphysics" Doctorate Program (1989) contains much information regarding the use of Meditation, and Self-Hypnosis for Metaphysical, as well as Clinical purposes. I will make many references to the material from this comprehensive program.

Methods

Most of the potential clients who approached me about Hypnotherapy as a means of altering unwanted behavior such as smoking, fear elimination, low self-esteem, and over-eating, generally, I have discovered, did not concern themselves with, nor did they necessarily believe in living a spiritual existence, nor did they particularly have an interest in, or belief in Metaphysics or Meditation. There was even a certain amount of skepticism on their part about the effectiveness of Hypnosis!

This is ironic, as daydream, Meditative, light-Hypnotic and "Alpha" brainwave-states have been scientifically measured and proven to be identical, according to Shields (1986). These potential clients were, however, generally on a *journey of self-improvement and growth*. Those who inquired about Hypnotherapy as a means of exploring past and between-life existences, discovering their angels and guides, etc., had a definite interest in things Metaphysical, we had observed. They, despite, belief in the effectiveness of Hypnosis, had sometimes requested Guided-Visualizations, and/or Meditations to accomplish all of this, instead of Hypnosis, because they did not realize that it is all the same thing, that is to say, the brainwave-state under light-

Hypnosis, is the same as a Meditative, and/or daydream-state, according to Shields. (1986) They sometimes doubted that they could be hypnotized, in which case I provided for them the statistics that only two- percent of the population cannot be hypnotized, as stated by Shields (1986). I then went on to explain and to define, in scientific terms, the hypnotic-state, comparing it to a daydream-like state, as stated by Hewitt (2004). We did suggestibility tests, as described by Hathaway (2003) or susceptibility test, as referred-to by Shields (1986), with these potential clients, which proved to both the potential patient and the Practitioner that they (the potential patient) could indeed be hypnotized.

They too, were on *a journey of self-discovery and growth*.

Those who had approached me to teach them Meditation, were more concerned with matters Metaphysical, as opposed to the logistical, problem-solving, areas of life, we learned. They generally, intended to use Meditation as a means of stress-alleviation and/or experiencing God. Often unaware of the other, *practical* benefits of Meditation such as improving self-esteem, stop-smoking, weight-control, lowering blood-pressure, etc., I attempted, occasionally succeeding, in educating them to these facts.

They too, were on a *journey of self-discovery and growth*.

It is interesting to note that although I had found in my private practice, both group settings and one-on-one, that, for the most part, all of the aforementioned, in regards to clients' requests and needs were generally true, there were some exceptions, although they were few and far between. I am grateful that my professional, as well as my educational background allowed, and still allows me, to provide the choices of either Meditation or Hypnosis for the potential client.

In regards to other professionals and/or Practitioners in the field of Metaphysics, teachers of Meditation and Clinical Hypnotherapists, I hope that there are exceptions to every rule, although, thus far I have yet to discover this. I can only, therefore, refer to my own professional experiences in regards to employing Meditation in place of Hypnosis, and vice-versa. That is, sometimes I (as a Clinical Hypnotherapist) will utilize Meditation/Guided Visualizations with a client to alter and improve their self-esteem, or even uncover several previous lives, for the purpose of the client understanding their true nature and purpose this time around. Hopefully other "professional" Clinical Hypnotherapists will also have the skill and leeway to accomplish this, if he/she is flexible enough to go with the wishes and belief-system of the client. Someone with little, or no Higher Education/degree, should not attempt any serious therapy with a client for legal and moral reasons. The skills necessary might not be present. This is why, I have found previous to my Clinical Hypnotherapy degree, for example, that practicing/teaching Meditation mainly for the purposes of relaxation, and/or contact with inner Higher Consciousness was acceptable and effective for everyone, as opposed to using Meditation as a means of "problem-solving", that is, altering unwanted behaviors and habits, for example, which is best left to a professional. It is even recommended, that to avoid potentially negative legal ramifications, that rather than, as a Metaphysician, one hypnotizes a client, or engages in "Hetero-Hypnosis," as Masters (1989) refers to it as, that they teach the client how to hypnotize themselves!

I will now discuss some specific cases and instances, where Meditation, Self-Hypnosis, and Hetero-Hypnosis were interchangeable for the particular needs of the client.

"Angela" (not her real name) was an attractive, educated, and motivated forty-year-old, with self-esteem issues due to her weight. She was working on losing twenty pounds, and quickly succeeding, when she approached me for Hypnosis for weight-loss. Although she had already been seeing a

Hypnotherapist for weight-loss, she was not getting the results she desired. She was somewhat skeptical as to the effectiveness of Hypnosis to begin with, and this was hindering her progress. I suggested that instead of Hypnosis, we could try Meditation as a means of allowing her to "let go" of past, hurtful events, and healing them through "Mind-Treatments Affirmations", as described by Masters. (1989) Furthermore, I suggested, that throughout the weekly Meditation-course that I was offering her, we would also do weekly "Meditational Programming Treatments", as described by Masters, (1989) if she would follow up with her own daily "Mental Rebirth Treatments", as provided by Masters (1989), that I would be teaching her. This, I suggested, would help her to rebuild her self-esteem while she was losing weight, so that she would never again eat to make herself feel good, but merely go inward for strength. In the process, the goal would also be to experience the Divine within. I mentioned that I would teach her a different Meditation technique each week, so that she could decide what worked best for her. She agreed. The first week, we started with the "Candle Concentration Technique" as described by Masters (1973), to get her used to focusing. One might say that we were doing a kind of Hypnotherapy/Self-Hypnosis program for self-esteem, and indeed, if we did say that, she psychologically wouldn't be open to it, because of the previous ineffectual Hypnosis experiences. The addition of going inward to experience God-Mind/Higher Consciousness/The Divine, etc. made the sessions both Western and Eastern Meditation, according to Masters (1989), as opposed to "Hetero-Hypnosis", as referred-to by Masters (1989) which would have necessitated the use of "Inductions" and "Deepenings" according to Shields (1986) to guide her into an Hypnotic-state, which she didn't want, regardless. As weeks went on, Angela felt better and better about herself, lost another ten pounds, and could now see light inside of herself with her eyes open or shut, reinforcing her faith/belief in matters Metaphysical! Upon completion of our weekly one-on-one Meditation course, Angela decided to join our weekly group-meditation evenings, which to this day she still attends. Angela's case clearly shows how Meditation was substituted for Self-Hypnosis, to effectively help her to improve her self-esteem, and eventually to help her to succeed in losing weight. Further on, you will see an example of Jeff's case, where Self-Hypnosis produced similar results, that of building positive self-esteem.

"Sally", (not her real name) one of my Reiki-students, approached me one day for Hetero-Hypnosis, as referred-to by Masters (1989) to help her release a past emotional trauma, which, she believed, prevented her from attracting and maintaining intimate relationships. Sally was a smart, ambitious, thirty-eight year-old, with a quick, and skeptical mind. The very fact that previously, she requested that I teach her Reiki, a Metaphysically-based system of energy-healing, was a breakthrough for her and her somewhat cynical and skeptical mind. She practiced Reiki regularly on others and herself, for minor issues. This day, she wanted to rid herself of an emotional obstacle that she believed was preventing her from living life to the fullest. She was also consciously aware of what the event was, which made it easier for me. I might have had to employ Hypnosis to also uncover this incident, which could have been locked deep within her unconscious mind, but not in this case. A lot of time and money would now be spared for her. Because she was aware of the relatively-minor event, I felt that this allowed her the luxury of choosing whether she preferred "Hypnosis or Meditation." She suggested Meditation, not because she was skeptical of Hypnosis, (indeed, her sister was successfully treated previously using Hypnotherapy) but because it felt "less rigid" for her. I agreed. Because this was "Meditation" and not "Hetero-Hypnosis", or one-on-one Hypnosis, as referred-to by Masters (1989), I didn't have to do a susceptibility test, as described by Shields (1986). She was already susceptible, willing and comfortable to my guiding her into an altered-state. The fact that she trusted me also helped. I could proceed, feeling unhindered by an Hypnotic-script, using only improvised guided-visualizations and getting her to focus on her breathing to accomplish what an Hypnotic Induction and Deepening, as described by Shields (1986), would do, which is guiding the patient gently into an altered-state of consciousness, or Meditation, which is the same brainwave-state as being in an Hypnotic-trance, or Alpha brainwave-state, according to Shields (1986). Others, like Hewitt (1997), also refer to this as a "daydream"-state. She had a positive emotional release, as opposed to a negative one, or "abreaction", as described by Shields (1986), which might have occurred had she remembered the actual event, "re-living it," and then letting it go; this is often as traumatic as the original incident. I have researched that in the long-term, this "re-living" and "letting go" does not benefit the patient, as the unwanted-symptoms caused by the original trauma, often return days, weeks, months, or years later. So why re-traumatize the patient in the first place? Sally slowly began to welcome into her life intimate relationships, which she has managed, to this day, to maintain, when previously, for her, this was either difficult or impossible. Sally's case was a successful example of employing Meditation instead of Self-Hypnosis or even Hetero-Hypnosis, as described by Masters (1989), for the purposes of the client re-empowering themselves by releasing a previous trauma. Similar results could have been achieved through Self-Hypnosis. Upon guiding the client into a Self-Hypnotic-trance, utilizing "Inductions" according to Hewitt (1997), "uncovering" methods such as the "Diagnostic-Scanning Technique", referred-to by Shields (1986), or "Free-Floating Regression", as taught by Shields (1986), for determining at what age, and specifically what trauma(s) occurred, and then eventually, employing Self-Hypnosis to "re-program" the person's thoughts and unwanted responses to the past trauma, as per Hathaway (2003). Teaching Self-Hypnosis to Jeff, a Computer-Technician, was more effective than employing Meditation, in his case, for building and maintaining, positive self-esteem.

"Jeff" came to me one day, at the suggestion of his friend, a former client of mine. It was my "Clinical Hypnotherapist" degree that made this particular method of self-help more palatable for Jeff, who "avoided New-Age stuff like the plague!" Jeff shared with me, on this particular day, the fact that at thirty-three, he avoided the singles' scene because he was too shy. As a youngster growing up, he was teased by his peers for being overweight. He had some how managed to conquer his weight-problem, but not his self-esteem issues. He dated occasionally, but expressed a willingness to date more frequently, and eventually get married, except that he didn't always have the "courage" to ask women out. Other than that, Jeff appeared to be a relatively well-adjusted, well-dressed, affluent, and educated adult. Self-Hypnosis for building self-esteem was one of my specialties; I even was marketing, at the time, an audio-CD for this purpose. Even if I would have been familiar with, at that moment, the benefits of teaching Meditation for daily Spiritual Mind-Treatments and Spiritual Mental Re-Birth Treatments, as described by Masters (1989), for the purposes of building positive self-esteem, it would still have been appropriate to teach Jeff Self-Hypnosis for building positive self-esteem. He just wasn't comfortable with anything else; he was even familiar with the scientific end of it all, including quoting sources on brainwave-states and their functions. After determining that Jeff was still a candidate for hypnosis, i.e.- a susceptibility test as taught by Shields (1986), involving his eyes shut tight with arms outstretched, palms up, at my voice suggestions that he imagine a helium-filled balloon was tied to one of his wrists, while in his other palm he held a large, heavy book; one arm went quickly down as the other went quickly skyward, confirming his suggestibility., as described by Hathaway (2003). As well, we determined that he had no contra-indications, as referred-to by Shields (1986), such as depression or anti-depressants taken within the last six-months. I proceeded with a series of long, guided-visualizations, or "Inductions", as well as "Deepenings," as taught by Shields (1986), to insure that Jeff was ready for this six-part therapy. For the Inductions and Deepenings, I decided to use the "sea-shore" and "stairs" visualizations, as taught by Hewitt (1997), initially employing some relaxation-exercises involving visualizing a mountain-top view and meadow, streams, etc. visualization, as described by Goldberg (1998). I suggested that Jeff will go deeper and deeper each time that he hears my voice, as suggested by Hewitt (1997), to reinforce that listening to the Hypnosis-CD I give my patients at the end of the last treatment, will work. Each time Jeff came for his session, I reinforced a particular positive-self-esteem suggestion, then taught him how he could, anytime, any place, hypnotize himself, giving himself any of the 24 positive self-esteem suggestions from the sheet I supplied him, as well. Jeff eventually went on to meet, date, and marry the "woman of his dreams", even starting a family. This was a case where Self-Hypnosis, as opposed to Meditation combined with positive affirmations, was the answer to someone building their self-esteem. I could have easily substituted (had I been familiar with, at the time) Meditation, Spiritual Mind-Treatments, and Positive Affirmations combined with Spiritual Mental Rebirth affirmations/visualizations as taught by Masters (1989), as in Angela's case, for Jeff's growth.

These previous examples from my case-files indicate how Meditation could have easily been substituted for Self-Hypnosis, and vice-versa, for the effective treatment/altering of unwanted behaviors of the particular patient. All that is really needed is the flexibility and education of both the practitioner and the patient.

Findings

Firstly, let's clarify the terms "Hypnosis", "Self-Hypnosis", "Clinical Hypnotherapist" and then "Meditation" "Hypnosis" and "Self-Hypnosis" are techniques that enable one to achieve an altered-state of Consciousness, (the day-dream state) deliberately, and direct one's attention to specific goals in order to achieve them, as taught by Hewitt (1997).

Strictly speaking, the term "Clinical Hypnotherapist" refers to one who has a professional degree in the area of hypnosis and psychotherapy, according to Shields (1986), and may apply this to help patients to rid themselves of unwanted behaviors such as over-eating or smoking, for example, by guiding them into a state of hypnosis using any number of "inductions" or visualizations. "Self-Hypnosis", according to Shields (1986), may be taught to the patient in order for them to relax more, boost their self-esteem, motivate themselves, and to support their willingness to not smoke, for example. This is accomplished by the patient guiding themselves into an hypnotic-state using their own inductions and visualizations. According to Masters (1989), for legal reasons, the Practitioner should only teach "Self-Hypnosis", rather than practice "Hetero-Hypnosis" i.e., Hypnosis induced upon another. As a Metaphysician and Clinical Hypnotherapist, I have found that employing "Hetero-Hypnosis" for uncovering the previous, and between-life existence of a client rewarding for themselves, as they discover in this way their soul's purpose in this lifetime. "Meditation", according to

Dr. Masters (1989), is accomplished by using one or more methods to withdraw the five senses and the mind from its attention to the world outside oneself and to make contact with the inner mental world of one's own mind. The popularity of Meditation in North America is thanks to the popularity of the Beatles in the 1960's and their teacher, the Maharishi Mahesh Yogi, whom they sought out for personal growth, according to Masters (1989).

Meditation may be divided into "Eastern", or Transcendental (experiencing the God-Mind within) and "Western", or using this altered-state to allow positive prayers and affirmations into one's unconscious mind for the purposes of improving one's "outer-self", referred-to by Masters (1989).

We would also like to clarify, at this point, the individual Hypnotic-states, and their relationship to each other.

Scientists, employing a device called an electroencephalogram or EEG, measure and define the various electrical-impulses put out by the human brain during its various stages of consciousness, described by Goldberg (1998). These waves emitted from the brain are measured in "cycles-per-second", or cps. For example, the wide-awake state, or "Conscious Mind Proper", as referred-to by Goldberg (1998), is referred-to as Beta, and is generally 14-20 cps; the "Subconscious Mind", as described by Goldberg (1998), or Alpha-state, is the brainwave-state that most Hypnotherapists desire to get their patients to, for it is the state that allows the patient to be the most open, or susceptible to, positive affirmations and suggestions, in other words, anything said to the patient while they are in Alpha-state will "sink-in" or stay in their subconscious mind. This is the same brainwave-state as "daydream state", and it is also the same brainwave-state as Meditation, although sometimes the Meditative-state will dip deeper, that is, into Theta, as described by Hewitt (1997). Psychic experiences sometime take place in Alpha, according to Hewitt (1997). It is generally 7-14 cps. Theta's frequency-range is generally 4-7 cps, and this is where hypnosis can sometimes take place as well, suggested Hewitt (1997). All of our emotional experiences seem to be recorded in this state, and is the special range where that opens the door of consciousness beyond hypnosis into the world of psychic phenomena. Theta is the range where psychic experiences are most likely to occur, according to Hewitt (1997). Total unconsciousness is measured at 0 to approximately 4 cps and is called Delta. Not much is known about this range, states Hewitt (1997). According to Dr. Michael Newton, best known for his "Life-Between-Lives" or "Soul Regression" work, states that there are actually three-levels of Alpha-state: (a) The lighter-stages, used for Meditation, (b) The medium stages, generally associated with recovering childhood traumas, is often useful for behavior modifications such as stop smoking, gaining/losing weight, etc., and (c) The deeper Alpha-states, where past-life recovery is likely to occur, according to Newton (2004). I personally employ Theta-stages for any kind of Past, and/or Soul-Regression work, in addition to stop-smoking and weight-control therapies. I generally employ Meditation (Light-Alpha stages) for behavioral modifications such as building positive self-esteem, which often leads the patient to losing weight on their own. My clients and I have made great strides towards their building their self-esteem through the use of Meditation, as opposed to say, the deeper-stages of Theta, during Self-Hypnosis, which have proven successful for the clients as well. It is often less intimidating for the client, if we use Meditation for the aforementioned purposes, as they may have some issues about being hypnotized, such as skepticism, according to Newton (2004), fear of staying hypnotized, or even of revealing personal secrets, according to Shields (1986).

There are great similarities in the methodologies used in entering into a Meditative, and/or Self-Hypnotic-state.

Firstly, in the initial stages of Hypnosis and Meditation, both attempt relaxation and concentration simultaneously, according to Masters (1989). That is to say, that a focal point of concentration may be utilized, (in Hypnosis, for example, a spiraling hypnotic-wheel, a point on the wall or ceiling, the sound of a metronome; in Meditation, focusing, with closed eyes up into your third-eye, or the use of a candle-flame) in order to achieve a mental-focus and thereby relaxing. I agree with Dr. Masters (1989) when he states that a Student of Self-Hypnosis is better at practicing Meditation, and a Student of Meditation is better at practicing Self-Hypnosis, because both students are used to the same basic initial methodologies for achieving relaxation and concentration simultaneously. It would, therefore, not be so unimaginable, (as stated previously) that if one were to walk down the hallway of an office-building where people were engaging in Meditation in one room and Self-Hypnosis in another room, that one might see a Meditation student sitting, gazing at a candle-flame, and likewise, the student practicing Self-Hypnosis gazing at a bright-light or a pendulum, according to Masters (1989). Both are using a "fixation-object" to concentrate their mind's energies or to achieve mental focus, for the purposes of relaxation. Insofar as the similar goals of Self-Hypnosis and Western Meditation are concerned, both are essentially concerned with improvement in one's outer self. We have already described how we have helped others to achieve this, employing either Self-Hypnosis or Meditation. Either methodology is as effective. The only limitations are those imposed by potential patients, or even the Metaphysicians or Clinical Hypnotherapists themselves, often because of the misinformation and lack of acceptance of Hypnosis by the medical profession until recently, and being branded "the work of the devil" by the Christian Science Church, as stated by Masters (1989), and the competence level of the Practitioner themselves, according to Shields (1986).

Recently, I came across a colleague's brochure on Hypnosis, in which I was delighted to find the quote: "All Hypnosis is Self-Hypnosis." This quote, I feel, takes away the potential fear surrounding Hypnosis, legally also shifting the emphasis from "Hetero-Hypnosis", as Masters (1989) calls it, to "Self-Hypnosis", desirable, according to Masters (1989), as previously outlined. A Clinical Hypnotherapist may insure the reality of this quote thusly: When utilizing susceptibility tests, for example, as taught by Shields (1986), one may determine whether the patient is: Suggestible to direct suggestions from the Hypnotherapist; categorized as "Authoritarian". In my opinion, undesirable, as the goal is always to have the client self-hypnotize themselves. B) Able to give themselves suggestions internally; categorized as "Permissive". Desirable, because they can tell themselves that it's okay to relax into a Meditative/Self-Hypnotic state, or Alpha using their own will and desire. C) Able to use their heightened imagination for entering into Self-Hypnosis/Meditation; categorized as "Creative". This is also desirable as they are using their own will/skills to enter into Meditative/Self-Hypnotic state. The more control of their own free will the client knows they have, and the more the patient participates in the "Induction"-process, the more in control of their free will they will feel they have, and the less fear and resistance they will have entering into Meditative/Self-Hypnotic state. The client may therefore, truthfully and accurately refer to the process as "Self-Hypnosis" which is more desirable, not "Hetero-Hypnosis", or "Hypnosis". Therefore, the statement "All Hypnosis is Self-Hypnosis" will promote the useful and legal concept/belief that the patient utilizes their own free will to enter into Meditation/Self-Hypnosis. The exception would be with patients who, for whatever reasons, need an authoritarian figure, and/or someone to tell them what to do. They would fall under the susceptibility category of "A", previously referred to above. These patients will willingly and more easily, in my experience, go with the verbal Hypnotherapy inductions/guided-meditations specifically designed to relax them into an altered-state, but strictly speaking, this would be categorized as "Hypnosis"/"Hetero-Hypnosis", not "Self-Hypnosis", in which case a waiver-form, signed by the potential client in any and all cases, could relinquish the Hypnotherapist of any legal and financial responsibilities, in the case of patient dissatisfaction, for whatever their reason.

I have described generally, initial methods for Hypnosis/Meditation common to both, as well as the goals common to both, but let me describe now, in greater detail, the techniques and philosophies that differ between the two, in other words, those that clearly differentiate between Meditation and Self-Hypnosis.

It is crucial that I reiterate, at this stage, what I said earlier about professionals, as opposed to non-professionals, utilizing Hetero-Hypnosis: unless you have some sort of recognized and legal degree/certification/license to practice Hetero-Hypnosis, I recommend against its practice. Employ Meditation. There are no legal requirements, nor are there any therapeutic promises or suggestions in regards to Meditation, other than for promoting relaxation, particularly, in general, with Western Meditation. Utilizing positive affirmations for strengthening self-esteem, in Meditative-state, will accomplish, as I have outlined earlier, just as much as the more lengthy, and costly, Hypnosis for Self-Esteem. If you are blessed enough to have a legal Hypnotherapy degree, then utilization of both, in one's Metaphysical practice, is most desirable, according to Masters (1989). Strictly speaking, the terms and specific "Inductions" and "Deepenings" techniques, as described by Shields (1986) are exclusively employed in Hypnosis and Hetero-Hypnosis, as opposed to Meditation; but the concentrating inwardly on one's third-eye, and/or mental/verbal uttering over and over of a mantra, or the focusing on one's breathing, as is employed in Meditation, also accomplishes the same goals of focusing and relaxing, but is not referred-to as an "Induction" and "Deepening", when discussing Meditation. Initially, according to Goldberg (1998), fixation-points such as a candle-flame, or spiraling hypnotic-wheel for relaxation and focusing may be used in Hypnosis, but Inductions and Deepenings as described by Shields (1986) or Hewitt (1997) must eventually be used to guide the subject into a deeper state of Hypnosis. Whereas, with Meditation, the repeated focusing inward, as previously described, results in achievement of the desired Alpha-state, required for both Hypnosis and Meditation. The reasons for the differences are cultural and scientific, that is to say, that Meditation came to North America via the spiritual-mystique of India, (as previously discussed) while Hypnosis and its origins were scientific: During the 1840s and 1850s, according to Hathaway (2003), Dr. Elliotson successfully treated patients for epilepsy, hysteria, headaches and rheumatism using Hypnosis. He also, during this time in England, performed over 200 painless operations, again, employing Hypnosis. A specific example of an Induction, according to Shields (1986) is a "Progressive Relaxation", where in the subject is asked to concentrate on relaxing each and every part of their body, one-at-a-time. Then, according to Hewitt (1997), a Deepening such as imagining oneself walking down a long and winding staircase, one-step-at-a-time, until one reaches the bottom is employed. A variation of this, according to Shields (1986), is the escalator, or lift (British word for elevator) method, whereby the subject is asked to "see" in their imagination, each numbered-floor lighting up in the elevator, as they are "descending lower and lower, deeper and deeper into relaxation". Of course, one might similarly state here that visualizations are often used in Meditation, which are sometimes referred-to as "Guided Meditations", whereby the Meditator is visualizing themselves walking on a beach, for example, which Hewitt (1997) also employs in Hypnosis. Again, the end result is common to both Meditation and Hypnosis: entering into the altered-state of Alpha brainwave state.

Discussion

The findings expressed within this essay will impact society in a number of positive ways, provided that these findings are willingly and truly attempted and practiced consistently by professionals in the field of Metaphysics as well as in the field of Clinical Hypnotherapy.

Although the individual levels of competency of these Practitioners will vary greatly due to varying academic and practical experience, in addition to the individualistic views, attitudes and personal perspectives of these Practitioners, in addition to their varying levels of skepticism and confidence, one must still acknowledge the measurable positive impacts of the practices should they be put into general use. For example, no longer will a patient be limited to the standard choices of treatments, Inductions and Deepenings offered by the Clinical Hypnotherapist, as outlined previously. If the patient feels more comfortable staring at a candle-flame, and focusing on their breath, or sitting cross-legged, mentally repeating an affirmation or mantra for the purposes of entering into an altered level of consciousness, as opposed to staring at a spinning, spiraling Hypnotic wheel, this would now be possible, for that same brainwave-state to be entered into. Conversely, if the patient feels at home with the more clinical methodology of watching that hypnotic spiraling wheel, versus having incense and New Age music playing in the background as they focus inwardly up into their third-eye, they now have that option for entering into an altered-state of consciousness. If someone wishes to experience their Past Lives, but they feel more comfortable in a more clinical atmosphere, then the Hypnotherapist may guide them into those realms using the more clinical methodologies of hypnotic-wheel, longer Induction and Deepening, etc. Provided that the Metaphysical Practitioner is licensed, and experienced to do counseling, they may effectively use Meditation in place of Hypnosis to aid patients in the areas of self-esteem, weight-control, smoking, current past-life traumas, etc. if the patient feels uncomfortable in a more clinical setting of the Hypnotherapist. That is to say, provided that the academic and legal qualifications of the Metaphysician are met, they may employ their Meditational treatments in place of the Clinical methodologies of the Hypnotherapist, and vice-versa.

This would impact society greatly, as the patient would now have more options and flexibility of choices, in regards to bettering themselves, with lesser personal limitations.

This would also impact society positively, as the professional Metaphysician and Clinical Hypnotherapist could now have greater choices and flexibility of methodologies, in order to assist patients in their betterment. Both the professional and the patient could potentially grow in experience and flexibility as well.

Ultimately, however, what will determine the broader use of these tools, will be the initial flexibility of both patient and Practitioner, as well as the general competency, and recognition of the Practitioner for the need of the use of a methodology not usually employed by them in assisting the specific individual needs, and catering to, the individual belief-system of their patient. Perhaps now, this essay will shed light on these possibilities, and societal benefits.

Summery and Conclusions

It should be clear now, as to what Meditation, Clinical Hypnotherapy, Hetero-Hypnosis and Self-Hypnosis are, the brainwave-state they have in common, as well as the techniques for entering into Self-Hypnosis and Meditative-state, common to each other, as well as differing from each other.

What is now uncovered, as well, is that either Meditation or Self-Hypnosis may be employed equally effectively, by either a Metaphysical Practitioner and/or Clinical Hypnotherapist, for improvement of one's outer self, potentially providing more services and flexibility, therefore, for the patient and/or Meditation-student.

Since Self-Hypnosis and Meditation have been shown, within the context of this essay, to be interchangeable in methodologies, brainwave-state and benefits, the title of this thesis, as well as the question, "Hypnosis or Meditation" have been realized and answered.

The only remaining issue that might persist in the mind of the Metaphysical Practitioner and/or Clinical Hypnotherapist, is not necessarily in the effectiveness of Meditation or Self-Hypnosis, but rather in that of their own competency in executing the methodologies. In addressing these personal doubts, we ask only that the regular and diligent practice and execution of Meditation and/or Self-Hypnosis be realized. As for the possible doubts as to the effectiveness of these modalities in actual and practical clinical or Metaphysical practice, we ask only that the Metaphysician and/or Clinical Hypnotherapist attempt interchanging their use, either in their own private research, or in practical, clinical use, in their own practice, for the purposes of educating themselves and others as to the effectiveness of these modalities.

Metaphysics, Meditation, and Self-Hypnosis For Better Living

It is at this point that I am including my previously-published e-book of the same title as this chapter, the purpose and reason being that it is important to have a grounding and knowledge-base in New Thought/Metaphysics and Spiritual Mind-Science/Theocentric Psychology to understand the differences between commercial (Western) Psychology and (Eastern) Metaphysical Psychology. With the former, one has more levels of the unconscious-mind to work with, and therefore heal, for maximum results. Enjoy now, "Meditation, Metaphysics, and Self-Hypnosis For Better Living".

Introduction

There are numerous definitions of "soul", and even more ways to access, understand, and commune with it! If you are looking for a book that in scientific terms defines "soul", this isn't it; choose, rather, to research it yourself, and then define "soul" for yourself! If, however, you can feel, and have felt profound joy and pain at any time in your life, and you want some more of that "good stuff" (while getting an education in the meantime), then this book is for you.
If you are searching for something "more" in your life, this book is for you.
If you are a "seeker" of truth, this book is for you.
If you seek to dwell in the "Upper-Room of Consciousness" or "Higher-Ground", this book is for you.
If you seek to encourage the unfoldment of your soul, your spiritual evolution if you will, and discovering your life's purpose, this book is for you.
 Understanding this "Science of the Soul" is crucial.

"Science" is proving and bringing into the tangible, through repeated testing and practice, a theory or the intangible.

This book represents soul (or spiritual, or metaphysical) subject-matter proven time-and-time again through my own and thousands of other individuals' efforts through testing, practicing, and then resulting in consistent proof. You now have in your hands this proof for your consideration and use.

This book represents the culmination of years of research, both clinical and otherwise, in addition to years of practice: watching and documenting the hits and misses, the successes and failures of my patients, clients, and students in this field of metaphysics. I've participated in many patients resolving their emotional issues, participated and witnessed healings occur physically, and I'm proud to say I've also certified and graduated several hundred as metaphysical counselors and practitioners/healers. Needless to say, through this work, I've increased my own, as well as others' quality of life. I'll never forget when I saw with my own eyes my patient's spine straighten out after years of them having scoliosis; the sight of a delighted (and much more mobile) patient's slipped-disk return to it's rightful position; even my own eye-sight improve greatly (this confirmed by eye-specialists without an explanation why) because of a shift of perception (pardon the pun).

Using a combination of psychology, intuition, hypnotherapy, some skill and knowledge, I have helped countless numbers (mostly documented by myself, some of whom appear in this book) to transform their lives (at one extreme) or lead a happier, more quality life (at the other extreme). They are now whole, healed, and complete emotionally and physically, thanks to the co-operation of their "soul" or spirit. A daunting task you say, healing the soul? Nonsense! Numerous and plentiful works by Plato, Aristotle, Lao Tzu, the Buddha, Jesus, Krishna, Quimby, Holmes, Freud, Jung, and many more have taught their documented techniques over eons of time. We stand on the shoulders of these giants and great minds of the past, sharing and teaching. The proof of the science of the soul is in the demonstrations and results, and now, it is within your grasp.

It is your turn to receive and to enjoy.

I am a certified and qualified Doctor of Metaphysics, (with a double-Doctorate: a Ph.D. in Mystical Research from the University of Sedona, and a Doctor of Divinity from the University of Metaphysics) Ordained Metaphysical Minister, and Clinical Hypnotherapist.

This means that using my learned knowledge of Holmes' philosophies, Quimby's "New Thought" techniques of mesmerism, Mind/Metaphysical/Meditative Treatments, conventional Clinical Hypnotherapy techniques, (rooted, as previously stated, in Quimby's "New

Thought" practices, in any case) and Metaphysical and Western Psychology. (which, as also stated, are based in the ancient wisdom and philosophies of the sages, plus Quimby, Jung, Freud, and the other contemporary therapists)

My intense education and experience in Hypnotherapy was gained through the Robert Shields College of Hypnotherapy, England. I am an Associate-Member of the Canadian International Metaphysical Ministry, member of the American Metaphysical Doctors Association, and member of the Association of Ethical and Professional Hypnotherapists. (England)

I have always had a profound "faith" in myself and humankind in general, regardless of what my personal experiences have been, or what the atrocities of the world still seem to bring onto itself. I believe that this (mostly) unyielding faith is essential in life, both for myself personally and professionally, as well as for others. This profound and consistent faith is another thing that qualifies me.

I have also counseled Pastorally/Spiritually/Metaphysically thousands of patients and clients. What that means is that I provided information, resources, and tools, all "God" or "spirit"-based. Whatever the person's definition/concept of "God" was is what I worked with; I have not yet, in my 15 years out of a total of 30 in the field of Metaphysics, as a Metaphysical Counselor, encountered anyone who had no belief in God, or some sort of a Higher, creative power. This is probably due to the very nature of the field I am in. Also, because I believed intuitively, as I still do, that we have all the answers stored somewhere deep within us, and I have always tried/try to guide the person to finding the solutions themselves, rather than depend on some outside source, be it another person, etc., thus they are truly self-empowered. Certainly I would be fooling myself and be less than truthful to you, if I denied my highly-developed sense of intuition, which always guided me to ask the "right" questions of the patients and clients in a session, thereby leading them to emotional breakthroughs, which healthier, happier lifestyle is based upon. This "intuition" I cannot and will not try to explain scientifically, but more "philosophically": it is "God-given". I cannot deny, that like the aforementioned P.P. Quimby, I could almost always, with more than ninety-percent accuracy, pinpoint what was troubling them on the outside, without them initially stating their issue(s) and with sixty to seventy-percent accuracy, pinpoint the emotional causes of their unhappiness; further probing and questioning would determine/confirm the usual childhood/adolescent/early adult traumatic reasons for their distress. Hypnosis and/or meditative treatments and techniques with "God the Healer" being the basis, thus far, has resulted in an eighty-to-ninety-percent "success" rate, or "healing" of past emotional traumas of my clients, as opposed to the more contemporary and commercially-accepted Clinical Hypnotherapy techniques. This is what qualifies me to write this book.

As a Clinical Hypnotherapist for a number of years, I have initiated self-hypnosis to assist my patients in improving their self-esteem, controlling their weight, and to stop smoking, among other things. These patients have reported a more than eighty-percent success-rate to me.

As a Doctor of Metaphysical Science, I have been also utilizing meditation in a similar fashion, because: (a) The Alpha brainwave state in self-hypnosis is identical to the brainwave-state during meditation, (Shields, 1986) and: (b) At the request of some clients, whom, for one reason or another preferred meditation over self-hypnosis. These same clients have also been reporting a similar success-rate to me as well, in the improvement of their self-esteem and for controlling their weight.

I have also been facilitated regular weekly "Mystical Meditations", the goal being for my students, clients, and patients to experience contact with the Divine within them, and also for eliminating their unwanted thought-patterns (Masters, 1989), for example, thoughts and feelings of lack, as opposed to thoughts and feelings of abundance and prosperity.

In addition to these regular meditation gatherings, I have facilitated weekly "Chakral Meditations", based on the works of myself, Dr. Masters, and Dr. Mishra's book "Fundamentals of Yoga", re-published in 1987. The purpose of this meditation being purely observational: during this "Yogic-Meditation", in which the students focus upon each of the energy-centers, or "Chakras" of their bodies, what occurs in their minds? Do they seem to reap any concrete rewards/results? Are these results/rewards purely metaphysical, clinical, or a combination?

As a Doctor of Metaphysical Science and Clinical Hypnotherapist, my goal is always to promote the independence and self-empowerment of my students and clients.

My background and expertise is in metaphysical/spiritual counseling, hypnotherapy, Reiki/metaphysical/spiritual energy-healing, and in an effort to help my clients, patients and students to "evolve" spiritually over the years and to just plain feel fulfilled, happy, and well, I have also combined my knowledge of philosophy and psychology to have written a number of "how to" books (one of which you are holding in your hands) so that I can go out into the general populace and speak with, and share these tools with more people on masse, rather than just one-on-one. Some call these lectures "Transformational Speaking".

My years of research and experience into the effects and benefits of various kinds of hypnotherapy and meditation (including "Fear Elimination Therapy" of which I am a certified Practitioner), and the "Mind Treatments" (which I now sometimes call "Alpha Quantum Therapy" ©TM) seems to make me something of an "expert" in the eyes and minds of some people. To these people I say, "It's the journey, not the destination."

Let me give you another disclaimer besides the one you just read at the beginning: traumas such as deaths, assaults, abuse of all kind, (including ongoing or those that have ended regardless of how recent or long ago) and shocks, (including large purchases such as home or car, bankruptcy, major life-changes such as births, marriages, first sexual encounter, relationships ending, regardless of how recent or long ago, personal and/or work betrayals, as well as losses due to fire, theft, etc.) all have several things in common.

First, they will impact on your self-esteem and sense of worth for an unspecified amount of time; there are no specific time-limits because everyone's rate of healing is different.

Secondly, you never really forget the rape, or the death, or the loss of the house, etc. The memory/memories become fainter and fainter, but they all never completely go away. Don't expect that any modality (alternative-wellness or conventional) will erase the event(s).

The feelings/emotions associated with the event(s) become less and less intense, but never completely go away either unless you recognize what they are, (anger, resentment, fear, etc.) and then deal with them in whatever healthy ways you choose to.

This is how this book can help you provided you want to do the work and really want to move forward. The Science of the Soul may provide some temporary coping-tools such as meditation, to first distract you from the feelings and emotions associated with the past incidents and/or events. The book will also help you raise your self-esteem/self-worth if you continually practice the methods here, such as meditation/self-hypnosis linked with affirmative-prayer/affirmations. The modalities mentioned in the book such as hypnotherapy can help you remember the event(s) if you've blocked them out, so that you can eventually work through the associated feeling/emotions. The modalities mentioned in the book such as Mind-Treatments and/or Fear Elimination Therapy will lessen or change to more positive emotions or no emotions at all, your traumas/events. Seek out any Alternative Wellness Practitioner qualified in the Mind Treatments and/or Fear Elimination Therapy, or see a conventional psychiatrist or psychologist if you prefer. I cannot support alternative wellness methods/modalities other than Reiki, Pranic Healing, and Theta, because I have had personal and professional experience with them; (I am a Reiki Master/Practitioner, a Pranic-Healing Practitioner, and I've had success as a patient with Theta) I cannot support any other alternative-wellness methods only because their effectiveness has not been proven to me, including modalities such as natural medicine; (herbs, etc.) this does not mean that other alternative wellness methods are ineffective, just that I cannot support or repute that which I have not tried.

If you cannot cope with your feelings, or if they are interfering with your day-to-day activities especially if the shock or trauma occurred more than six months ago, then you should go for conventional psychiatry, psychology, or therapy. If the conventional methods don't seem to work for you, alternative wellness or complimentary medicine could be more effective. I especially advise seeking professional help, whether it be conventional, alternative, or complimentary, if you are still troubled by shock or trauma more than six months old. If you cannot remember the specifics of the trauma, I (or any qualified hypnotherapist) can help jog your memory so that you can start to heal the associated emotions. If you remember the trauma(s) then I (or any qualified Alternative Wellness Practitioner) can help heal the associated emotions using the Mind-Treatments or Fear Elimination Therapy. (not to be confused with E.F.T.)

One more note: references and source material referred to generally herein ie) "(Masters1989)", or "Masters (1989)" have the specific reading material/sources including the publisher listed at the back of *The Science of the Soul* under "Suggested Reading".

I hope this book helps you in your own self-evolution and happiness at this point along the road of your life, and that you keep passionate, happy, and fulfilled along your way.

The Spirit and the Soul: The Real "You"?

An Emphasis on the "Spiritual" and the Scientific!

All this title really means is at this point I'd like to really "dig into" what I've been referring-to as your "spirit", "soul" and emotions, in other words the "Spirit" part of "Mind/Body/Spirit", since it is so utterly and obviously tied into the feelings and emotions of happiness. "Spiritual" in this case will in no way, shape, or form have any religious connotations, but in actuality scientific!

Metaphysics: Philosophy, Science, or Superstition?

One way to explore and understand the all-important "soul" and "spirit", which we previously-referred-to as the "emotional-guidance system" or "happy-gauge", if you will is by way of what some call "Spiritual Mind-Science", "Mental Science", "Science of Mind", "Religious Science", or "The Science of Spiritual Psychology", often classified as "Metaphysics".

Again, is "Metaphysics" a philosophy, a science, or a superstition?

Metaphysics as a Philosophy

According to Herman J. Aaftink, the Founder-Director of the Calgary Life Enrichment Centre, and author of *Brand New Me: The Art of Authentic Living*, "metaphysics" is the popular name for the ancient philosophy of Idealism, first taught by Plato and Aristotle about 2,500 years ago. Metaphysics means "beyond physics": it is the attempt to present a comprehensive, coherent and consistent account of reality, of the Universe as a whole, including ourselves. **Metaphysics** is also referred to as a branch of Philosophy that deals with First Cause and the Nature of Being. It is taught as a branch of Philosophy in most academic universities today under the label of **"Speculative Philosophy."** According to Aaftink, metaphysics acknowledges a "cosmic", or "Universal mind" (or "God-Mind") as the operating principle of order and change as well as the source of all existence.

Dr. Paul Leon Masters, the Founder/CEO of the two oldest and most respected Universities of Metaphysics in the world, the "University of Metaphysics", and the "University of Sedona", both being two of my Alma Maters, states that the word **"Metaphysics"** has become a description of many fields of interest. When one expresses an interest in **Metaphysics**, that interest may be in any one or a combination of the following subjects: Philosophy, **Religion**, Parapsychology, **Mysticism**, Yoga, ESP, Dreams, Jungian Psychology, Astrology, **Meditation, Self-Help Studies, Positive Thinking**, Life After Death, Reincarnation, etc. The common denominator of these and all similar subjects deals with an exploration of Reality, and in the idealistic sense, how such knowledge may benefit human life on this earth, both individually and collectively. According to Masters, if, then, this is the aim of such interests, it is why most professional **Metaphysical Practitioners** (that is to say, Practitioners of Metaphysical Counseling and Healing) regard **Metaphysics** as a **Spiritual Philosophy** of life. All but a very few **practitioners in Metaphysics** today have a pivotal point of some sort of **Spiritual Philosophy** in whatever system or teaching of **Metaphysics** they are engaged. If we were to travel from one **metaphysical teacher** or organization to another, we would find people engaging in different things, all under the label of **Metaphysics**. This could be a wide range, such as yogis, mystics, astrologers, positive thinking teachers, **meditation teachers**, grapho-analysts, **spiritual healers, self-help teachers**, etc. The range is wide, but again the basic denominator is the search for truth, purpose and meaning in life, which cannot be isolated from basic spiritual questions.

The basis for most of these beliefs/perspectives come not only from the ancient Greek philosophers, but also the Hindu mystics, ancient mystical/esoteric Buddhist teachings, and even the Taoist "Immortals" who created the now-popular Qi Gong, Tai Chi, and Kung (or Gong) Fu practices of meditative breathing and gentle physical exercises for health and longevity, in China. Swami Vivekananda, a Hindu mystic who lived from 1863-1902 is considered to be largely responsible for bringing Yoga, again, a series of deep-breathing exercises and poses as a means to maintaining and increasing health and longevity, as well as union with the divine, to Europe and to America, while the Maharishi Mahesh Yogi, another Indian mystic made popular by the Beatles in the 1960's, is considered responsible for bringing "Mystical Meditation", whose purpose is Divine-contact/union, healing, and health-maintenance, (as opposed to "Western" or "Guided Meditations" which are mainly for relaxation, and for eliminating unwanted behaviors/habits) to the west.

I will be referring to "Metaphysics" from the perspective of the practice of "Western" or "Guided Meditation", self-hypnosis, as well as "Eastern Meditation" mainly, within this book, as the basis for health. Again, you may look at this as essentially using the relatively untapped potential, or "power" of the human mind, with self-hypnosis or meditation being the key to tapping, exploring, and/or opening it. Therefore, one of the main aims of this book is not so much working with metaphysics from a "speculative-philosophical/spiritual" perspective, but more from a practical and clinical perspective, and thereby supplying to the reader potential tools for healing and health-maintenance through the power of the mind.

Science has already for many years measured and acknowledged health gains as a result of the practice of Western Meditation and self-hypnosis for, among other things, stress-management, (which encourages greater psychological "peace-of-mind") reduced high blood-pressure, increased physical stamina, etc.

The benefits of meditation and self-hypnosis has long been scientifically acknowledged in the treatment of weight-loss, improving self-esteem, stopping/discouraging unwanted habits such as smoking, etc. (Hewitt, 1997)

I will be outlining some of my own research results/experiences with my various clients as a Clinical Hypnotherapist and Doctor of Metaphysical Science, to further underline the point.

As far as any clinical "proof" of divine contact/union, doctors and researchers such as Newberg and D'Aquili in their book *Why God Won't Go Away*, (2002) show brain-scan images of subjects taken while they are meditating and while they are not. The scans taken during meditation show increased activity and blood-flow to the front part of the brain, which is usually involved in focusing attention and concentration, is more active during meditation. This makes sense since meditation requires a high degree of concentration. The **second image** shows that there is decreased activity in the parietal lobe. This area of the brain is responsible for giving us a sense of our orientation in space and time. One could hypothesize that blocking all sensory and cognitive input into this area during meditation results in the sense of no space and no time which is so often described in meditation, or the term for union with the divine as "no-thingness" in Zen meditation. (Reps and Senzaki, 1998)

Metaphysics as a spiritual way of life will be discussed later in this book, including reflections on contemporary spiritual movements such as "Christian Science" (founded by Mary Baker Eddy, a former patient who was "cured" by P.P. Quimby), "Religious Science", or "Science of Mind" (founded by Ernest Holmes) and "Unity", also grew out of Phineas Parkhurst Quimby's practice and studies of the 1850's.

Metaphysics as a Superstition

Since metaphysics is largely looked upon as a philosophy, and not necessarily as a science, let's look at it firstly as a superstition.

"Superstition" is defined in the Webster's dictionary as "An irrational belief; any practice inspired by such a belief." Also: "An unreasoning belief in an omen, supernatural agency, etc." As just outlined, the basis of metaphysical beliefs are thousands of years old, and much of the aspects of it (such as the therapeutic benefits of meditation) have long-since been proven by science, as will be outlined shortly. Even the developer of the science of spiritual psychology, Ernest Holmes (The Science of Mind, 1988) likens metaphysical science to mixing paint-colors: essentially it doesn't matter who mixes, say red with yellow, the outcome is always orange; or mixing blue with yellow, the outcome is always green; the outcome is always the same, similar to the law of gravity: whoever throws something in the air is guaranteed that the object will descend toward the ground! The outcome is always the same; metaphysics is not an irrational or unreasoning belief with a superstitious or unproven basis: most of the therapeutic effects of metaphysical practices have already been scientifically proven, and much more of it is still being proven even to this day!

Therefore, metaphysics is not a superstition. It may have started as a spiritually-based philosophy thousands of years ago, but is now grounded in scientific proof.

Metaphysics for Health

The more "practical" application of Metaphysics as a means to better health and healing was rediscovered by the aforementioned Phineas Parkhurst Quimby on the east-coast of 19th century America, via his study of "mesmerism" (or hypnosis), which in turn became the basis of modern-day Clinical Hypnotherapy and Psychotherapy, including "Transpersonal Psychology". Self-hypnosis was later employed by the famous therapist Sigmund Freud on his patients, who, along with Carl Jung, (metaphysician and therapist) also analyzed patients' dreams as a means of understanding their unconscious mind, wherein theoretically was stored the basis to ill-mental, emotional (and in Quimby's belief-system, physical) health. The manner in which Quimby employed a combination of psychology, theology, intuition, and mild hypnosis and meditation, was also the basis for "NLP", or "Neuro-Linguistic Programming", a now-popular form of psychotherapy made popular and associated with Milton Erikson, although NLP was actually co-created by 3 men (Grinder, Bandler, Pucelik) and developed by many others (Steve and Connie-Rae Andreas, Robert Dilts etc). Erickson was among several that were modeled by the creators (including Satir and Perls), where modeling is the actual basis of NLP... over the decades there has been some rumors and subtle change of perception, and now people equate NLP with Ericksonian hypnosis, which is at best a partial truth. Many also believe that Quimby also contributed to Beck's creation of "Cognitive Therapy". We will discuss in detail later on Quimby's methodologies, comparing them in practical terms to some contemporary therapeutic clinical methodologies, my own clinical use of all methods, as well as how the reader may practically employ some of these methods for improving and maintaining health.

What I partially intend to explore in the context of this book are the results of these two meditational groups, in order to outline the workings of the human brain, and more specifically, the human mind; how emotions created by memories rooted deep within the memory-banks of the brain, or mind, affect the day-to-day quality of our life, including goal-setting and health. Comparisons of meditation and hypnosis will follow, as will theological, psychological, philosophical, and metaphysical perspectives and discussions on the implications of defining the existence of God deep within the human brain or mind, and finally how this "God-Power" may be harnessed to encourage optimum health overall.

Initially, I intend to discuss the experiences and responses of my meditation students, based on the practical research I have done through questions, answers, and discussions with the two separate meditation groups over the last year: what are their experiences (visual, auditory, etc.)? Do they feel/believe they have/are achieving union with the Divine, and if so, why do they believe this? For example, what are the experiences? What other things do the students feel that they are achieving through meditation? How is this manifesting? For example, relaxation, evolution of their soul, progress in their day-to-day lives, etc. Is their intuition (or

Divine-guidance) increasing, thereby placing them in a "Divine-Flow" of their soul's purpose/synchronicity of life-events, etc.? How is this being proven to them? Has the quality of their life overall improved, and if so, in what ways? Do they believe that they are having any paranormal/psychic experiences during meditation, and if so, what are those experiences? For example, experiencing past-lives, angels, guides, etc. How do they feel about these paranormal experiences?

Are my students succeeding in the concrete or clinical realm/arena, such as in weight-loss, improved self-esteem, etc.?

Next, what will follow will be a discussion of these answers, and their implications: How useful from a Clinical Therapist's perspective have these experiences been?

How useful from a Metaphysician's perspective, for example, in professional use as a Doctor of Metaphysics, have these experiences been?

As stated earlier, I will ultimately describe the various processes which have improved the quality of my patients' and clients' lives. They are all happier and healthier on all levels. My recent use of "Mind-Treatments", loosely based on Quimby's techniques, and not dissimilar to the aforementioned treatments, have further increased the percentile of healed patients!

Thus, in writing this book, I intend to emphasize for other Metaphysicians and Clinical Hypnotherapists, as well as for the broad public, the importance/benefits of meditation from a clinical, as well as spiritual/metaphysical perspective, as well as how these findings may affect society as a whole.

The Human Brain-A Primer: Metaphysics as Science

The Organ

We will not define the human brain right now, in detailed, scientific, and biological terms. We will discuss in detail further on in this book the brain as a processor of perceptions.

At this point, we choose to refer to the human brain as the computer of the human body. It is that which stores up memories and events that have occurred in the person's physical environment. It is not necessary that we describe how the brain processes the physical senses such as sight, smell, etc., nor do we deem it relevant that we describe the processes of the brain which allows such things as motor-skill movement. In the words of Swami Vivekananda in Volume 6 of "The Complete Works of Swami Vivekananda", he states, "The Ophthamalic Centre in the brain is the organ of sight, not the eye alone...only when the mind reacts, is the object truly perceived." In other words, it is enough that the brain is the true processor, or computer, if you will, of that which our human senses perceive; it is our brain that rights the inverted-images that our eyes see. It is our human-mind that subjectively perceives an event in our life to be positive or negative; it is our memory-bank, or "Personal Subconscious" part of our brain that stores events that occur in our life, and what Jung called the "Collective Unconscious" part of our mind that transforms people formerly and currently in our lives into mythological-like "gods" or "goddesses": good or evil characters on an unconscious-level, based on, again, the human-mind part of our brain.

All that we will concern ourselves within the context of this book, is firstly the brain's function as it is relevant to memory, and perceptions of memory, and secondly, the duality of the human brain in regards to creative and emotional function versus the reasoning, logical part of the brain.

Science has already proven that one half of the human brain processes logic and reason, while the other hemisphere concerns itself with the function of creativity and emotions.

Recent scientific research in Wisconsin has also determined that the stress hormones produced within the brains of monkeys have been proven to be the cause of the emotions of fear and anxiety.

Getting to the Scientific/Clinical Sources of Fear and Anxiety

Wisconsin emotion researchers have been studying defensive behaviors in monkeys to better understand the related temperament that may put humans at risk, including extreme shyness, excessive anxiety and exaggerated fearfulness. The researchers have found that chronically fearful and anxious monkeys have specific patterns of brain electrical activity as well as elevated levels of two kinds of stress hormones. Their latest study challenges the existing theory that the brain structure called the amygdala controls all fear and anxiety responses. The findings show that in primates, the amygdala is involved in acute fear responses, but doesn't appear to play a role in anxiety responses that may be present from early in life and related to general temperament.

Brain Responses to Antidepressants

A new drug called venlafaxine is proving to be very successful clinically in treating depression, but how exactly does it affect brain function? This study uses functional magnetic resonance imaging (FMRI) techniques to establish how antidepressants such as venlafaxine can reverse the brain alterations that are associated with depression. The study also explores how treatment with medications may change depressed patients' responses to positive and negative stimuli.

Fearful Temperament Points to Vulnerability

The free-ranging male monkeys of Cayo Santiago, a small island off Puerto Rico, provide a unique opportunity to study biological factors associated with different kinds of emotional and social styles because they normally go through a highly stressful event during adolescence that results in death for 25 percent of them. UW researchers have identified monkeys for whom this process is especially difficult and have found that the animals have fearful temperaments as well as specific brain activity and hormone levels related to elevated stress. Additional physiological measures will be taken to learn which constellation of factors may make some monkeys more vulnerable to stress and more susceptible to disease than others.

Meditation and the Brain

In this small but highly provocative study, the UW-Madison research team also found for the first time, in humans, that a short program in "mindfulness meditation" produced lasting positive changes in both the human brain and the function of the immune system.
The findings suggest that meditation, long promoted as a technique to reduce anxiety and stress, might produce important biological effects that improve a person's resiliency.
Richard Davidson, Vilas Professor of **psychology** and **psychiatry** at UW-Madison, led the research team. The study, conducted at the biotechnology company Promega near Madison, will appeared in the Journal of Psychosomatic Medicine.
"Mindfulness meditation," often recommended as an antidote to the stress and pain of chronic disease, is a practice designed to focus one's attention intensely on the moment, noting thoughts and feelings as they occur but refraining from judging or acting on those thoughts and feelings. The intent is to deepen awareness of the present, develop skills of focused attention, and cultivate positive emotions such as compassion.
In the UW study, participants were randomly assigned to one of two groups. The experimental group, with 25 subjects, received training in mindfulness meditation from one of its most noted adherents, Jon Kabat-Zinn, (Kabat-Zinn, a popular author of books on stress reduction, developed the mindfulness-based stress reduction program at the University of Massachusetts Medical Center.) This group attended a weekly class and one seven-hour retreat during the study. They also were assigned home practice for an hour a day, six days a week. The 16 members of the control

group did not receive meditation training until after the study was completed.

For each group, in addition to asking the participants to assess how they felt, the research team measured electrical activity in the frontal part of the brain, an area specialized for certain kinds of emotion. Earlier research has shown that, in people who are generally positive and optimistic and during times of positive emotion, the left side of this frontal area becomes more active than the right side does.

The findings confirmed the researchers' hypothesis: the meditation group showed an increase of activation in the left-side part of the frontal region. This suggests that the meditation itself produced more activity in this region of the brain. This activity is associated with lower anxiety and a more positive emotional state.

The research team also tested whether the meditation group had better immune function than the control group did. All the study participants got a flu vaccine at the end of the eight-week meditation group. Then, at four and eight weeks after vaccine administration, both groups had blood tests to measure the level of antibodies they had produced against the flu vaccine. While both groups (as expected) had developed increased antibodies, the meditation group had a significantly larger increase than the controls, at both four and eight weeks after receiving the vaccine.

"Although our study is preliminary and more research clearly is warranted," said Davidson, "we are very encouraged by these results. The Promega employees who took part have given us a wonderful opportunity to demonstrate a real biological impact of this ancient practice."

Davidson, who is integrally involved with the **Health Emotions Research Institute** at UW, plans further research on the impact of meditation. He is currently studying a group of people who have been using meditation for more than 30 years. His research team is also planning to study the impact of mindfulness meditation on patients with particular illnesses.

My Own Research

Following is information based on feedback received from my students of meditation over the course of a year. Their names and specifics were altered to allow for their anonymity.

Allan is a forty-something male in the entertainment industry, who until a year ago, had little previous experience with meditation and spirituality. I informally met him one day through a workshop a colleague of mine was facilitating. Allan's motivation for joining both of our newly-formed Mystical Meditation, and Chakral Meditation groups, was to "open" his third-eye; in his words, to "Develop latent psychic abilities." I sensed initially that he was a natural-born healer, that is to say, with God's help he could initiate the self-healing of others. I told him this, and I also referred to him as an "Earth Angel", which he seemed to resonate to. I use this term "Earth Angel" solely because it seems to intuitively "open" people up to understanding the idea of "being there for others", for a "greater purpose" or "service". My motivation with Allan was to help him to see that "psychic abilities/paranormal experiences" are merely a rung along the step up the ladder to being one with God (Masters, 1989); that union/contact with the Divine within us should be the primary goal, with everything else being secondary. I let him know this, just to be clear as to my own motives. He agreed to participate.

This meeting of Allan coincided with the time I e-mailed an invitation to the Mystical and Chakral Meditation-nights at our home, to my existing clients, patients, and students. Our rather large living-room comfortably accommodates twelve people, so I wasn't worried about how many would attend.

Immediately after this e-mail invitation was sent out, Ellen, a 22-year-old unemployed female, expressed interest in attending, as well as Lucy, a forty-something Legal Secretary, both of whom were patients of mine. I felt that these individuals were relatively diverse in education and background, had no previous formal experience in meditation or self-hypnosis, and that it would be interesting to hear what their feedback was with this meditation. What they all shared was a decided interest in matters metaphysical: Ellen was reading many popular self-help books, and Lucy had experienced some paranormal activity, specifically those with spirits and ghosts allegedly, in the home she shared with her husband. She also wished to do healings with animals, which was what motivated her to be my Reiki-student as well. She also had a profound faith in God. Allan was the Reiki-student of that colleague of mine, who referred him to me.

The first evening of our weekly Mystical Meditation night, I made it clear that the primary purpose was union with the Divine. The secondary purpose was to re-program any unwanted or negative thought-patterns, eventually replacing them with thoughts of prosperity, health and abundance. Anything extra gained/experienced during these nights was a bonus, I added, and that at the very least, it was their "quality" time of feeling peace and relaxation from their busy day/week. I asked them to not expect anything concrete or specific-just to enjoy. Then, I asked them to close their eyes and imagine that they are looking up and into the centre of their brain, where their Pineal-gland resides. The Pineal gland (also called the Pineal Body, Epiphysis Cerebri, or Third-Eye) is a small **endocrine** gland in the vertebrate **brain**. It produces **melatonin**, a hormone that affects the modulation of wake/sleep patterns and photoperiodic (seasonal) functions. (Wikipedia 2008) I sometimes refer to this as the "interior-region of their head", rather than the "brain", as it sounds less clinical.

Traditionally, though, during Yogic/Kundalini-Meditation, one of the major "energy-centers" or "Chakras" is traditionally referred-to as the "brain". (Mishra, 1987) The basic, clinical concept being that when one attempts to stimulate their Pineal gland, using whatever method, that hormonal-secretions created by this, stimulates a series of sensations which may be interpreted as "spiritual" or Metaphysical". These "experiences" are often linked with union with the Higher Self/God/God-Mind.

It is not the purpose/goal of this paper to debate the validity of this.

Further, it has been noted, from a clinical perspective, that focusing up and slightly back, (towards the brow-area) with or without eyes opened or closed, induces a light-meditative state. (Shields, 1986) This is sometimes why, as Hypnotherapists, we ask the subject to focus (with their eyes open) up and back towards a spot on the ceiling, or on the tip of a pencil/pendulum/pocket-watch, etc. held over their heads. After a minute or so, their eyelids do become heavier, as their eyes strain back to focus on that point.

The three attendees were then asked to sit with their backs straight, (to facilitate the flow of Kundalini-energy; clinically, to enable an easier, deeper breathing) and with either their feet planted firmly on the ground or their ankles crossed, (which ever felt more comfortable) to simply "relax" and "let go".

I clicked on the meditation music, and began reading from my script. Technically-speaking, the first ten-minutes is an "induction" (Shields, 1986), or script designed to take them to "Alpha" or meditative/daydream brainwave-state, perfect for relaxation and therapeutic uses such as re-programming unwanted thought-patterns (Goldberg, 1998). In my Hypnotherapy practice, I have a tendency of taking my patients to a deeper "Theta" (or near-sleep) brainwave-state, useful for Soul-Regression (Goldberg, 1998) and Past-Life Regressions, so I felt somewhat insecure about guiding them only to Alpha, fearing that it wouldn't yield any results. I quickly remembered how incredible my own personal meditative experiences in Alpha-state have been for almost thirty years, so this then calmed any concerns I had. The next twenty-minutes consisted of some of the affirmative meditations for re-programming unwanted thought-patterns, which I had studied in my Ministers/Bachelors program from Dr. Masters' course, (Masters, 1989) and the last five minutes was from a script designed to "bring them back" up and out from "Alpha" to wide-awake state, or "Beta"-state. (Hewitt, 1997)

The feedback that followed this initial meditation greatly surprised me.

Allan described a purple light in front of him, and a feeling of heat and vibrations in his hands which he attributed to the flow of the healing-energy known as "Reiki". Lucy described the identical experience, while Ellen went into a detailed account of having "seen" her "animal guides", describing a black panther and other large, protective cats that she had seen around her during the meditation. I asked her how this made her feel, and she said "good" and "protected". I let her know that these visions are from God, confirmations of His protection of us, but she insists, still to this day, that they are her "animal totem" or "animal guides". I feel that if this belief empowers people, it is not for me to argue/discredit them. Clinically, I believe they are archetypes we carry deep within our unconscious-mind, in other words, how we really see ourselves, and our strengths. Interpreted thusly, in her case, she unconsciously feels she has the strength, loyalty and tenacity of those big cats. The final result is the same, regardless: self-empowerment.

Over the next six months, all three attendees seemed to move forward in their individual lives: all attracting jobs/careers/love-lives that gratified them; Metaphysically, I attribute this to the Divine-contact accomplished during meditation, which allowed them to, among other things: (a) Open a channel to becoming more Intuitive, or God-guided day-to-day, thereby allowing them to be at the right place, at the right time, with the right person(s) for the receiving/initiation of their prosperity (b) Improve their self-esteem, through these healing, meditative "Mind-Treatments", (Masters, 1989) thus allowing them to make changes in their lives with greater courage, confidence, and conviction, and (c) by being more God-guided, they were living more and more their "soul's purpose(s)", that is to say evolving more in a positive, healthful way, to be more and more of "service" to others and to themselves. Clinically, I attribute this to the attendees gaining greater self-esteem and confidence through the suggestions made during the self-hypnotic/meditative-state. (That they are stronger, healed, happier, etc.) They are more prone to hang onto these suggestions subliminally, in their subconscious mind, via the suggestions given under hypnotic-state.

Lucy, for example, almost a year later, is now making a great deal of money in her spare time doing Reiki on animals, so much so, that this income may soon replace her full-time Legal Secretary position! She is richer financially as well as emotionally and spiritually. She attributes this to the Divine-contact made during the Mystical Meditations.

Allan has a clearer vision of what he wants to do: he has been acquiring more alternative-wellness modalities, with the hopes of eventually leaving his full-time job and starting a wellness centre. He, too, attributes this to a "oneness" with God he feels and experiences during this meditation.

Ellen appears to be more "employable" in the material-world, supplementing her government check with part-time, non-metaphysically-related work, and is happier and emotionally healthier. She believes that this is due to the contact with God she has during the Mystical Meditations.

Overall, they seem to have a stronger base of God, and are far more confident.

In this almost twelve-month process, they have also been experiencing much more, during the Mystical Meditation nights, which by the way, now consists of as little as five, and as many as ten people regularly attending on the Wednesday-nights!

Ellen's experiences seem more elaborate, consisting of "journeys" to places she describes in detail, usually "floating" over, around and through these places in her visions. Many times, she is "underwater", with a dolphin as a guide, other times she "sees" multi-colored fields with fountains and/or mountains, her black-panther guiding her all the way. She has seen people she recognizes from this lifetime, understanding the purposes for them being in her life now.

The therapeutic aspect of meditation for her is undeniable, far quicker, and less expensive than if I would hypnotically regress her to these "past-lives".

This would suggest that meditation definitely has therapeutic benefits, as well as potentially being a substitute in many cases for hypnosis.

Allan's experiences, although less dramatic on the Wednesday, or Mystical Meditation nights, are if anything, consistent. He continues seeing light, either purple or green, symbolically representing to him healing and protection around him, as he has expressed.

Lucy often sees either what she perceives as "angels", and/or souls from previous lives. I've explained to her that our soul carries past-memories from previous lives in its Astral-Body (Masters, 1989) and meditation opens up a channel, enables her to "see" and/or remember these souls. Clinically, although I've also explained to her that the "angels" and "guides" are unconscious extensions of the strengths she carries of herself in her unconscious-mind, which are also physical manifestations of God, she prefers believing that these are actual angels and guides. She also claims to see her deceased mother around her, often times during meditation-periods. This makes her feel loved, protected, empowered, and hopeful. Who am I to argue with this? When she first began meditating, she did not have any of these experiences. Her desire to "grow spiritually and psychically" continues to be satisfied, apparently. From an emotional and psychological perspective, I believe this to be all positive. Her self-esteem has grown ten-fold, compared to when she first started, showing me that the re-programming-to-abundance aspect works, and is just as effective for self-esteem issues as is self-hypnosis is, in my private practice. She has gained the confidence to approach strangers/potential clients and customers for her animal-healing business. From a spiritual, as well as psychological perspective, the Mystical Meditation nights are definitely working, and are still growing.

The Thursday-night Chakral Meditations yield fascinating results as well.

I had originally written this guided meditation to encourage an activation of the energy-centres known as "Chakras" within the body, and then to document the results in my students. Many of the students from my Wednesday-nights participate, but we also have attending several who exclusively attend only the Thursday nights, because they generally prefer the "feel" or "energy" of the Thursday nights over the Wednesday nights. I have given everyone a chance to experience both nights, and now we have a consistent attendance over both nights. Some attend both nights, others attend only one or the other for the reasons just outlined: the "feel".

I will now proceed to describe the experiences that Ellen, Allan, and Lucy have on the Thursday-nights, (which are significantly different from their Wednesday night experiences) in addition to those experiences of Greg, Helen, and Janet on the Thursday nights. Greg, Helen, and Janet have tried the Wednesday nights, preferring the Thursday nights, while Ellen, Allan, and Lucy attend both nights.

Greg is a twenty-two-year-old ad executive, who has studied Reiki with my colleague and teaches yoga at a local outlet. He is satisfied with the Reiki-modality and is seeking to expand his wellness business, which includes the selling and promotion of a multi-level marketing nutritious fruit-drink. He is confident and well-adjusted.

Helen is a housewife and Reiki-Practitioner, lacking confidence, but attending meditation to build her self-esteem; although she regularly attends Thursday nights and my Sunday morning Metaphysical service, she does on occasion attend Wednesday nights. She is fascinated with the paranormal, but leans towards the mystical, spiritual, and healing-aspects of life.

Janet is a forty-something housewife, mother of two grown children, and book-keeper. Fascinated with the paranormal and highly intuitive, she originally approached me to attune her to Reiki, so that she could help others to self-heal. Having lost her father-in-law last year to cancer, she believes she feels his spirit around her. Her goal is to be able to see him and all spirits/ghosts, so that she might help the living with closure. This is her primary motivation for attending our Thursday night Chakral Meditation, although time allowing, she also attends the very occasional Wednesday night meditation, again, preferring the "energy" to Thursday night's meditation. She believes her psychic abilities will improve through regular meditation. She is also a strong believer in God, so I need not emphasize meditation as a means to union with the Divine with her.

Much like the Mystical Meditation, there are three parts, consisting of the aforementioned "induction", middle-part, or focusing one-at-a-time on each energy-centre and resting in the experiences of each one, and finally concluding with the wrap-up/guiding back up and out to the external world once again. During the period of time that I have been conducting the Chakral Meditations, the results have been dramatic for all.

All see "other-worldly" places and people they do not recognize.

The experiences are always of a paranormal nature, as opposed to the Mystical Meditation's revelation/spiritual/God-oriented experiences of peace and tranquility.

They all claim to have had these experiences during the phase of the meditation when they are asked to focus either on their naval, and/or brow/centre-of-their-brain area.

Both Greg and Lucy have seen very clearly an "eye" in front of them. During this experience, they have attempted to see into the iris part, but this yielded little results, that area appearing clouded thus far. I told them that this is like a mirror into their soul, and when they are ready, they will begin to see clearer. Clinically-speaking, both Greg and Lucy are intellectually-driven, with a strong literary background; to them, the "eye" subconsciously represents a certain level of spiritual-evolution they unconsciously feel proud of, therefore the "eye" physically manifests to them as a symbol of this evolution. When they believe, deep-down, that they have evolved even more, spiritually, they will no doubt be able to "enter into the iris", and even begin having experiences from that perspective. I don't feel it is necessary to share with them, at this point, the clinical explanation, as psychologically it might squash their enthusiasm and confidence to delve deeper.

All parties still experience glimpses of what they believe are past lifetimes; they base this on the manner of dress of the characters they are seeing. They believe these characters/personalities they are seeing to be people they know now, and have known before, and will know again. I explained this metaphysically to them: during these Chakral Meditations, they, in their oneness with their Higher-Self/God, etc. are in the Eternal-Moment: past/present/future all exist at the same time; I further explained that this is how "Psychics" operate, at least those Mystically (or God)-oriented: in slightly altered-state, they can access that divine/eternal-moment, where glimpses of the past/present/future reside, in order to share the information gleaned from this experience with their clients, or in other words, by giving them a "reading". This explanation seems/seemed to satisfy the attendees intellectually. I added that the "Sleeping Prophet", Edgar Cayce, claimed a similar theory: that Psychics, during meditation, can apparently access the unconscious desires of those they are reading for, since we are all in one Mind of God, and the one Mind of God resides within us as well; this is much like the then-popular New Thought beliefs that are now re-emerging as well. I also reiterate about Jung's theory of archetypes/visual metaphors of ourselves which reside in our unconscious-mind: could these people they glimpse during meditation represent various aspects/strengths/weaknesses of their own personality/character, thus enabling them to self-analyze and improve? I encourage them to do this.

These visions of past-lives during the Chakral Meditation-nights by the participants generally fascinate, entertain, if not encourage them to return, time and time again. If this attendance and participation in meditation results in them enabling their spiritual oneness with the Divine, thus creating a more God-guided ability amongst them, then I, too, am satisfied, feeling that I am accomplishing a greater purpose.

All tend to also see angelic-like figures as well, giving detailed descriptions of hair-color, dress, sex, etc. Again, I refer to Jung's more clinical explanations for this, but I also ask those experiencing these angels, what and whom they feel they represent to them, to get them to self-analyze and improve themselves.

Ellen's journeys are far more detailed and elaborate on the Thursday-nights, however, they are also "case-book" Jungian experiences: unconscious metaphors for fears/concerns in her conscious day-to-day living, and I continue helping her with these observations at other times via metaphysical consultations.

Lucy still feels she sees her deceased mother-in-law. I never discourage her about this, as long as she feels empowered by these visions.

Helen and Janet feel vibrations in their hands and warmth which they believe to be Reiki, Helen sees white-light, while Allen continues to just see purple and/or green-light and the Reiki-sensations.

In summation, vivid colors, lights, symbols, tingling in their hands and nose, all of this and more have been experienced by the students of either the Mystical or Chakral Meditations. In their earnest efforts to evolve, my various meditation students who faithfully continue to attend these regular, weekly gatherings, are still experiencing these glimpses, which are both fascinating and encouraging to them. Many still insist that they are seeing their "angels" and "spirit-guides", past-lives, etc.

The conclusions I have come to thus far, based on the total almost a year's worth of observation and questioning of the attendees of the regular Mystical and Chakral-Meditation are this: generally, they seem to be intellectually and emotionally satisfied with these experiences.

The Wednesday night, or Mystical Meditation nights yield spiritual/God-oriented results/experiences, and have helped to improve the quality of the attendees lives via their improved self-esteem. The oneness with God that occurs, whether they are consciously aware or not, at the very least, benefits them spiritually.

The Thursday night, or Chakral Meditation nights afford more paranormal/psychic experiences. These have generally resulted in an "entertainment value" for the attendees, as they continue to faithfully attend weekly for these experiences. All believe that their psychic abilities have improved as a result of participating on the Thursdays, many of them describing specific experiences.

Again, I am thankful that they are also having Divine-contact/union, allowing them all of the aforementioned benefits of this.

The Findings

As just described, my meditation-students' experiences are wide and varied, but I can sum them up thusly: 99% believe they are making contact/union with God. The reasons for this are mainly because of the conscious experiences they are having, for example, the green or purple lights they are seeing. 30 % of this 99% who believe they are achieving Divine-contact are having these purple or green-light experiences. Of this 99% as well, the other 30% are seeing an "eye", white-light, a "brushing up against them" of something. This 60% of conscious experiences are convincing the 99-percentile that they are making Divine contact. Those believing they are consciously making Divine-contact feel relieved, protected, excited/enthusiastic.

One can sub-divide this 99-percentile into those who believe they are having some sort of paranormal experience, into the various paranormal experiences that they are apparently experiencing. Approximately 20% are seeing what they believe are their angels, guides, and/or animal-guides. They clearly describe the sex, hair-color, manner of dress, and style/color(s) of wings, if any! They describe what manner of beast (lions, bears, black panther, etc.) they have "seen" around them as well. They describe a feeling of excitement and satisfaction at this. Another 10% believe they are seeing their own Past-Lives, and describe the environment, manner of dress of others, even who they believe these people are in relation to their current-lifetime! This provides amazement, enthusiasm and relief that they apparently have an understanding of who they are now, and why others have reincarnated again into this lifetime. Less than 10% believe that they are "seeing" during meditation either into alternate dimensions/astral-worlds of the dead (where they describe clearly a dearly-departed, who gives them reassurance), or a past-life on "Atlantis" where they describe vivid images of molten-like, or fluid-like multi-colored fields, mountains, and red-skies! They will often describe the architecture as resembling early/ancient Greece/Rome. The people they encounter often resemble those they know in this lifetime, however dressed in ancient Grecian/Roman garb. Often, they will "ride" on a "dolphin" through air and sea! This makes them feel amazed and bewildered. They wish to draw and/or paint these images. Within this less than 20% are those who believe they have travelled, during meditation, to alternate "worlds"/dimensions, perhaps of an "extraterrestrial"-realm. They describe non-threatening "alien-beings" which makes them feel both curious and uncomfortable. It is the appearance of these aliens (either large, insect-like creatures, or the often-described diminutive, grey-skinned, large-eyes/head creatures) which makes them feel uncomfortable. They also vividly describe exotic vegetation and flora which apparently exist on these worlds.

Regardless of this subdivision of paranormal experiences, those involved completely feel safe "in God's hands" and/or believe that God is giving them these experiences for reasons as of yet unknown to them. Regardless, they feel positive overall.

Upon further questioning of the attendees to both the Mystical and Chakral Meditations, all feel relaxed and happy. Ten-percent feel that they are "on-track" with their "soul's purpose" or why they are really here, incarnated into this life. They believe that they are here to help others to heal themselves. It is encouraging to note that another 40% are passionate about entering into, or having recently entered into, the healing arts/alternative wellness. These 40% had been working at other jobs/careers that they no longer felt passionate about, are now achieving a modicum of personal, if not professional/financial success.

All attendees feel an overall improved quality of life, since regularly meditating over a year, noticing that there is more of a "flow"/synchronicity. They all, too, feel more relaxed overall, and speak of responding to situations, rather than reacting. Most are speaking of increased self-esteem and confidence, more readily going for that new job, relationship, situation, etc. when previous to regularly meditating, they would have hesitated or not pursued these things at all.

I must note here, that from a therapeutic or clinical perspective, my hypnotherapy patients have been making quicker progress in the areas of improved self-esteem, and/or weight-loss. That's not to say that the meditation students are not making progress in these areas, merely slower. It is my theory that because my hypnotherapy patients come to me with a focused intention of altering some unwanted behavior in their life, within a specific and finite time-frame, that they succeed quicker. With my meditation students, the lessening of unwanted behavioral patterns occurs as a "bonus" or after-effect, if you will, because the students' main goals with meditation are Divine-contact and paranormal experiences, without specific deadlines or time-frames.

Only 2% of my meditation students have lost weight significantly, mainly as a result of relaxing more, and feeling better about themselves, thus altering slightly their lifestyles and diet, naturally and gradually. Many have stopped/slowed-down smoking naturally, again, as a result of feeling better with meditation, as opposed to taking in that smoke. As for things like major addictions to drugs and alcohol, I have not yet personally encountered patients or students under this category.

Finally, based on the findings/results of a year's worth of observation of the Mystical as well as Chakral Meditation students, that the mind/body/soul benefits for these students (that is to say emotional/psychological, financial, spiritual) have far exceeded any expectations I, or they, might have initially had.

Discussion of Findings

What exactly are the implications of these findings? How can these findings affect society as a whole? What are the implications of these findings both from a clinical as well as a spiritual and metaphysical perspective? How might the Metaphysician as well as the Clinical Therapist benefit professionally? Similarly, what are the potential benefits, physically, emotionally, and spiritually for the clients of Metaphysicians and Clinical Therapists long-term? What are the potential benefits, physically, emotionally, and spiritually for the clients of Metaphysicians and Clinical Therapists long-term?
What follows now, will be a discussion of this.

Based on the findings previously outlined of my students of both types of meditations which I facilitated over the past year, it is encouraging to note that regardless of what specific experiences, feelings, etc. the participants were having, that Meditation is definitely a "gateway" to Metaphysics, as is Yoga. (Masters, 1989)

Whether it is "Western" Meditation, (Masters, 1989) whose primary goals are relaxation and/or elimination of unwanted thought-patterns, such as negative self-esteem, or "Eastern Meditation", or "Mystical Meditation", (Masters, 1989) whose primary objective is union with the Divine, all the subjects expressed enthusiasm to go on and regularly attend, due in part, to the experiences they were having, which due to a curiosity factor, created a drive about continuing, and/or because of their desire to be the best they can be. ie-develop spiritually. Regardless of their motives, the mere act of meditating would encourage a therapeutic, healing effect on a mind/body/soul level, whether they were consciously aware of this or not, in addition to evolving spiritually. (Masters, 1989)

The fact that many of them have gone on to study a number of other healing-modalities, such as Crystal and Theta healing, and Lomi Lomi Massage, which they have stated, was as a result of their own positive meditative experiences, their motivation being to help themselves and others, is also encouraging. One of them has even gone on to specialize in using Reiki to help animals to heal, all because of her "increased sensitivity" to apparently knowing what those animals feel, or an increased "empathy", if you prefer.

Allan's apparent increased ability to "see" or "know" more, which he attributes to regular meditation, encouraged him to study the Theta modality, which he is excelling at, he informed us. He claims that he can "see" the non-physical trouble-areas of the clients, due in part, he credits, to meditating regularly: again, an increase in psychic/paranormal abilities and empathy.

Whether it is because these Meditators are becoming more easily one with the Universal-Consciousness, (Seale, 1986) and therefore "knowing" tandemly what the clients are "knowing" unconsciously about what they are really needing, and/or whether they are merely increasing their own sensitivities on one level or another, is not important: they are nonetheless feeling encouraged to evolve spiritually, and to help others.

Because this study only involved people already open to/interested in the study of the paranormal and spirituality, it is difficult to arrive at conclusions to society as a whole, in regards to those who are more of a "clinical" nature. Perhaps as the general public is exposed to movies and television that depict the paranormal and spiritual in a positive light, (as of these writings, there are numerous television programs and movies about mediumship and ghosts) perhaps this will be a gateway, if you will, for the broad public to lean towards exploring these areas, Meditation being one direction; we can only hope that they explore it from this perspective of the "Mystic", (God-centered) rather than the short-term/superficial "Psychic" (paranormal) perspective.

Nonetheless, from the Metaphysician's perspective, it is obvious how the use of Meditation (both Eastern and/or Western) benefits their patients, if they prefer Meditation over Hypnosis: improved self-esteem, exploration/healing of the mind/body/soul, even weight-loss; it is a gateway to more matters spiritual, and thus, increases the patient's odds of evolving/healing on all levels. At the very least, Meditation provides relaxation/stress-management.

From the more clinical Therapist's perspective, Meditation accomplishes all that Hypnotherapy accomplishes, without the conscious aim of healing the mind/body/soul: it still reconditions the mind to function in a less dysfunctional/neurotic manner, by getting to the "root-causes" of the unwanted behaviors, just as Meditative Mind-Treatments heal the traumas in the Personal Subconscious which are the "root-causes" of the limited/limiting thoughts/behavior of the patient. (Seale, 1986)

It is not important whether the Meditators in this study continue on from a Metaphysical perspective, or move towards a more clinical Therapist's perspective, as long as they employ Meditation and/or Hypnosis as part of the treatments of their patients; this way, the clients will be ensured at least of a base of spirit, or God, which is the basis of all true healing. (Masters, 1989)

Results

According to all these findings, it is easy to see how Meditation provides satisfaction for the Metaphysician, as well as potentially, for the more clinical therapist. The sensations, visuals, etc. experienced during Meditation, encourage even the most jaded, clinical person to at least consider the concept/possibility that more exists beyond the known five senses, especially when they know what scientists and medical doctors have proven: that under hypnosis or meditation, the mind cannot make up things!

How can one argue, then, the validity of the experiences of these people, places, lights, symbols, sounds, etc., etc. during Meditation, Western or Eastern? How can one dispute the existence of anything more than the five senses, when the implication, therefore, of these experiences, being real, exist deep within the unconscious mind, where, according to Jung, we have stored symbols, archetypes and concepts of ourselves? (Masters, 1989) In other words, a greater Knowing/Understanding of ourselves exists deep within ourselves, within our unconscious mind. This has already been long-proven. That through the "key" of hypnosis, or meditation, (again, which scientists have proven to be the same brainwave-state) the unconscious human-mind may be opened, and thus, explored. How can anyone argue, therefore, that through this "tapping" if you will, of the human unconscious-mind, be it through Meditation or Hypnosis, that any and all dysfunctions, problems, and traumas exist, and may be uncovered and healed?

This is not a new concept: sages throughout time have spoken of this; in modern times, Freud, Jung, Quimby, have all spoken of and/or proven that through opening/contact with the unconscious human-mind, limitless potential exists.

Whether it is through the techniques of Self-Hypnosis/Hypnosis or Meditation which make direct contact with the unconscious levels of the human-mind, it does not matter. A greater understanding of one's Self occurs; even a healing, mind, body, and soul, occurs. Whether the patient describes past-lives they are seeing; whether they recall a trauma from this life or a previous one; whether they are enjoying a journey of the mind, and are seeing exotic places, meeting familiar or new people, animals, or angels and guides; whether they are taking time to focus in on the energy-centers, or "chakras" within their body; whether they are seeing a light, color or colors. These experiences specific and unique only to them, serve merely as encouragement, an acknowledgement by their unconscious-mind, a sign-post if you will, that they are on the right track. Even if the experiences are not always positive, it is still created by God, deep within them, so that they may explore these experiences, and heal themselves with God's unconscious guidance. Sometimes we call this unconscious guidance gained/developed through regular Meditation, "Intuition". A greater development of one's intuition is another sign of one's spiritual growth through Meditation. Even paranormal/psychic experiences are signs of one's spiritual growth, gained through meditation/self-hypnosis/hypnosis.

It does not matter whether the clinical Therapist formally employs Western or Eastern Meditation or not, as part and parcel of the modalities/services they provide; it is, as already stated, to the benefit of their clients that they at least do provide Hypnosis, Self-Hypnosis, or Hypnotherapy as a form of treatment for uncovering unconscious issues. Hypnosis has certainly become more widely accepted and used in recent times; (Masters, 1989) so has Meditation, even with a minority of clinical Therapists, who now often recommend it to their patients as a form of stress-management, as do many corporations encourage it on their employees breaks; and certainly with most Metaphysicians, as part of their practice.

The broad, general public has embraced Meditation more and more in recent times as well, since the Maharishi and the Beatles brought it to the attention of the west in the 1960's. (Masters, 1989)

Whether it be the private person, professional or non-professional, the Metaphysician, or clinical Therapist personally or professionally employing it, Meditation/Hypnosis continues to grow in popularity, providing a key to the wonders of the mind and the universe, through the exploration of the Universe within the Mind.

4 SCIENTIFIC/AFFIRMATIVE-PRAYER

We've thus far discussed in great detail the workings of the human as well as Universal Mind and how to access both through self-hypnosis as well as meditation for the purposes of healing as well as one's spiritual evolution. I'd like to tackle another component to New Thought/metaphysics, another spiritual technology known as "Scientific-Prayer" (the term coined by Ernest Holmes) a.k.a. "Affirmative Prayer", followed in the next chapter by "Prayer Treatments". The reason being is that all of these access the Universal Mind for prayer as well as for healing. Again, I have chosen excepts from my book, "Mystical Wisdom Complete" for this purpose entitled "Real Prayer: Petitioning or Affirming?"

There's not a person on this planet who hasn't heard of prayer. Everyone prays at some time or another, except of course, atheists. People pray in times of perceived need, others pray in times of joy, in gratitude. Everybody who prays will agree: some of their prayers have been answered, but not all of them. Why is this so?

To answer this, we must delve into the whole nature of prayer, and its mechanics.

In order to even consider praying, we must first believe

that there is some sort of chance that our prayer will be heard, and then answered. Somehow, whomever hears this prayer (usually God, or a Higher Power of sorts) will answer our prayer and help us or others. Of course, somehow everyone's prayer gets listened-to or heard, after all, God is omniscient and can do this! But why are some people's prayers not answered? Are some more important than others? Do some people take some sort of president over another? Why, why, why?

In my books, "Speaking Thoughts Into Existence" (ISBN-10: 1517327148 and ISBN-13: 978-1517327149) and "Scientific Prayer" (ISBN-10: 1512183717) I address the topic of spiritual prayer, if you will, as mere cause-and-effect, sort of like the natural results of a combination of visualization, faith, and belief. In reality, the primary ingredients of Scientific-Prayer/Prayer Treatments is faith: so much faith, that in fact you must believe, feel, and live as though your prayer has already been answered. This is the key. Apparently some indigenous people pray for rain (successfully) by silently standing outside, visualizing and feeling as if it is already raining; they feel the sogginess in their shoes and the drops upon their bodies; they can smell the moisture in the trees and bushes, they can hear the drops upon the leaves and ground, and they stand rejoicing, embracing this imagined downpour as they silently pray a prayer of gratitude for the rain! The key to this is their not only seeing, (visualizing it) but more importantly feeling it, believing it, accepting it as reality.

We can and have previously broken down the steps of Scientific Prayer: Oneness/Identifying, (with Universal Mind) Denying/Proclaiming/Affirming, Releasing, and then Acceptance. In essence, becoming one with God during Mystical Meditation, and then feeling gratitude, peace, love, joy, denying the condition that supposedly is, (say, poverty or illness) finally proclaiming otherwise, (the desired result, for example wealth or well-being) releasing this out, and accepting that it is already so in the Mind of the Universe, with feelings of great euphoria, relief, etc. This method may be used for distant healing of someone as well, such as in a Meditative Treatment/Prayer Treatment with the patient residing elsewhere. One merely visualizes the patient, and/or during meditative-state, looks at their name/birth-date, etc, and then declares them well with all of the emotion as if it is already so. Similarly, one may bless someone (either in person or at a distance) by visualizing a white-light at their head and heart, with two corresponding white-lights at your body, while in meditative-state.

Nevertheless, this is a prayer not of petitioning, advocating, and pleading, but a prayer of proclamation, affirming, and acceptance that it already is.

I have spoken previously about knowing what to pray for; if one is poor, obviously one prays for a job and money; if one is sick, one prays for health; if one is lonely, then they pray for love. All of this is also subject to karma: you may be prone to having less money or being lonely because of previous lifetimes' cause-and-effect, or karma. This can be corrected by affirming (during meditation) that you've sublimated negative karma for God's Perfect Light and Love. You must make sure that you're always affirming this, as well as affirming that you're releasing your personal ego-will to God, that you Identify with God, and that your prayers are coming from the Mind of God on a continuing basis during meditation, as meditation will powerize these affirmations or statements; then and only then do you have a chance at successful prayer. In traditional prayer, this would be the case however, in mysticism, one handles things thusly: if one is poor, one gives money to those more needy, (as if you already have an excess) one helps another if they cannot help themselves due to poor health; one makes a friend if one is lonely, and so forth, in other words, start to live as if you are already abundant in whatever particular area that concerns you. This is only part of it, although it is a great part. The greater part is knowing what to pray for!

The regular earthly shortcomings that our personal ego-will is more than aware of will come and go: money will be made and spent, friends and lovers will come and go, one's health will rise and fall. If you are regularly practicing Mystical Meditation, you will notice that the ups and downs have become less extreme. You are beginning to place importance on other things in your life, such as the well-beingness of others! This is called Universal Love, (or humanitarianism) and as you become more and more grateful for just being alive, the emphasis will be less and less on yourself, and more and more on helping others. It is as if, thanks to meditation, you have a Higher Perspective of life, and this perception is starting to motivate and drive you more. You may even be starting to use your Intuition (God Guidance) to lead you to where you should be, with whom, and what you should be doing! You may even start to discover some God-given skills and talents that previously you were unaware of. This God Guidance or Intuition will guide you to what you should truly pray for, with the chances therefore increasing for you to get what you prayed for since it came from the Mind of God and God knows what you have need of before you even know. It is the same as you not getting (necessarily) what you want, but really what you need! Did you ever wonder why, after praying for something, you actually got it, and then it was gone after some time, or you couldn't afford it? That's because your personal ego-will decided for you what you thought you wanted or needed, and it somehow materialized. The things that our personal ego-will materializes never is long-lasting; whatever God materializes for us, is. It's as simple as that!

You see now how crucial it is to pray for what God wants for you, and the way to this knowledge!

As long as you allow God to guide you to what you really need, the more your chances of your prayer being answered and to you keeping whatever it was the Universe manifested for you. This is the exact opposite of that popular DVD "The Secret": we don't tell God (the Universe) what we want, we open ourselves to know what God wants for us! Let your Intuition guide you, and you'll never go far wrong.

How does one discern whether it is wishful thinking or actual God-Guidance/Intuition? Only time proves this, and unless you were born with a higher-than-average degree of spiritual E.S.P., you must practice regular, ongoing Mystical/Contact meditation, and over time your Intuition will develop to a reliable degree. You will begin to see this more and more over time. Trust God to lead you to what you need, and you will have it!

5 PRAYER TREATMENTS

A Prayer Treatment is the compact, abbreviated-version of a Scientific-Prayer, but is no less effective!
It is a kin to blessing as well, but differs slightly from it in that you are not necessarily visualizing God's Light at yours and your subject's brow and heart-areas while affirming.
You might use a Scientific-Prayer/Spiritual Mind-Treatment with a patient seated or laying right in front of you, whereas your Prayer Treatment may not necessarily have a specific target and be more general.
An example of a Prayer Treatment for prosperity would be:
Oh Lord-in-me, whose light and love envelopes me, I affirm that already you are providing for me, allowing me ways to be guided to be with the right person, at the right time, to receive my prosperity! This knowledge and wisdom I acknowledge is already mine in the Mind of the Universe, And So It Is!
An example of a Scientific/Affirmative-Prayer for prosperity would be:
I close my eyes and turn away now from the outer world that surrounds me to enter into the innermost world of my own mind, body, soul, and spirit, to that Christ-Mind point of contact, where my soul is in an eternal state of oneness with the mind and spirit of God. Here in the Light of Higher Consciousness within myself, I recognize that prosperity is already mine, and I sit in this joy, happiness, and contentment knowing that it is already so in the Mind of the Universe! Any blocks, hindrances, and obstacles to my riches and prosperity are gone! Oh, I feel it to my bones! In gratitude and appreciation, I release this word, letting it be so now and forever more, and So It Is!
The wording of the Scientific-Prayer might even be a little longer, allowing for your patient to go deeper into altered-state, which must be in order for the prayer to be effective. Also feelings as if one is already prosperous, along with a faith, knowing, and conviction must be present as well for effectiveness. The Prayer Treatment being shorter, doesn't, by its

very nature, allow for an entering into of meditative/altered-state, but the feelings of conviction, faith, and knowing make it just as effective as the Scientific-Prayer, just shorter.

Use a Prayer Treatment if you are giving a metaphysical or Theocentric lecture, as a brief interlude and to place emphasis onto what you just said. You can begin and end with your Scientific-Prayer, as you are guided to.

Here are some examples of Prayer Treatments for specific purposes; feel free to use them, as they will go deeper than you expect while accessing the Universal Mind for a shift of consciousness as well as thought.

Worthiness

The key to many emotional issues, I have discovered over the years, lies in worthiness. When one doesn't feel worthy of love, or success, then their entire demeanor, attitude, and emotional state will not support love or success; in fact, this energetic-state will not support, nor encourage success in any area or endeavor! In fact, this energetic-state may even drive away any potential success of any kind.

Whether this negative attitude was learned through one's environment, (parents, teachers, co-workers) or through karma, not identifying with one's Higher Self, and seeing things through the eyes of one's ego-self, this may be remedied by reconditioning the unconscious mind through self-hypnosis or Mystical Meditation. Essentially one begins to re-program any unconscious beliefs hindering one's progress in life. This eventually results in the person realizing that they are worthy of success in all areas of their life, therefore no longer unconsciously hindering the process of success; one no longer sabotages any modicum of already achieved results.

Practicing the following exercises will allow one to re-program one's unconscious mind, thus giving one more of a chance to develop more positive self-esteem and worthiness, clearing the way for success. Say each affirmative treatment three times: first time, out loud, then silently to yourself, and finally just read the meditative treatment allowing each one to enter into the unconscious level of your mind, closing your eyes.

I Am Worthy

At this point, I am going to provide you with some affirmations, or more precisely, "re-programming affirmations" to be used in conjunction with self-hypnosis and/or meditation, in order for you to bring up your energies/vibrations to that of abundance, joy, and ultimately for stronger self-esteem so that you may more easily manifest.

I recommend that you get yourself quiet, enter into a self-hypnotic or meditative-state, (as previously stated) and then give yourself these suggestions/affirmations regularly. Early morning and/or before retiring at night is best, but anytime that you are in a slight meditative-state and therefore open to the suggestions will work well. I personally have typed some of these onto a recipe-card which I carry on me at all times. Laminating it will further preserve them for you.

General Re-Programming Affirmations

"My conscious mind is ruled by the power of the Higher Consciousness of God this day."

"Anything that appears to go wrong this day is immediately corrected and made right by the unseen Power of Source working through me this day."

"I expect unexpected good things to happen to me this day and every day."

"I am at peace this and every day, all day, calm, knowing that the power of Source and the Universe prospers me."

"My path is clear because Source lights the way for me."

Prosperity Re-Programming Affirmations

"In my Oneness with Source, I attract all that I need for my prosperity."

"I am joined already with the prosperity that I need."

"I am directed by Source to be in the right place at the right time, with the right person, for the receiving of my prosperity."

Spiritual/Faith Re-Programming Affirmations

"Every meditation brings me closer and closer to the reality of abundance and health in the centre of my mind."

"I am that which I am, and that which I am is Source, in the centre of my mind."

Now What?

I would like to provide you now with more affirmations, designed to program you subconsciously for success. An alternate way of absorbing these is to listen to these affirmations (just before falling asleep), which you have recorded onto tape or CD.

Success Re-Programming Affirmations

"Source properly directs the use of my time each day, timing my heart, soul, and mind for success."

"My mind is open every day to receive creativity and success from Source."

"Source directs my intellect each and every day."

"Each day I affirm deep within myself, in the core and nucleus of my Higher-Mind, that my life is turned over to the loving care of my God/Source-Mind."

"The thought of the Power, Peace and Love of Source within me replaces any thought of sadness that may enter into my consciousness."

"I communicate to others through the Presence of God at the core of my being."

"If someone is interfering with my achieving success, I bless and release them with all good wishes for their good and spiritual growth and continue along with my life."

"As the Divine helps me, I help myself, by taking action in every opportunity that life affords me."

"Failure is a process which has brought me one step closer to success."

"I am worthy in all ways because I carry the Presence of God's Strength, Wisdom and Love in the centre/core and nucleus of each and every day of my life."

Use all, or some of these. Whichever you feel might benefit you.

Troubleshooting

Here we will briefly fine-tune and discuss some things that might come up during your growth.

Sadness is an emotion that may still be coming up for you.
Distract your mind by going within (meditating) and experiencing Source-energy, and the sheer joy that experience will bring you. Also, get into a regime of physical exercise: this will improve your physical as well as emotional state. A diet high in protein and iron will elevate your mood. Also drink lots of water, and supplement your diet with vitamins such as B50, vitamin c, calcium and magnesium. If you live in an area where there is much rain, and/or cloudy days, you may find that Light Therapy works for you. These are portable rows/banks of lights that simulate sunlight, and may be place next to you when you are working. I have found that many people's lives have improved as a result of this therapy. You may purchase such lights by going onto the Internet and researching the words Light Therapy. While in a light meditative-state, give yourself the aforementioned affirmations.

Lowered self-esteem is still there; you feel a lack of confidence to just go for things.
Traditional counseling and therapy might work, in addition to Hypnotherapy for self-esteem. Try the affirmations we provided previously. Remember that someone once said, "We don't solve our problems, we outgrow them."

Nothing appears to be progressing, and/or progress is slow. This is normal. Sometimes weeks or months will pass, and nothing is materializing. This is a test of your faith and endurance. Most people will give up, but not you, because you know that your mind, body and spirit is adapting to, and integrating the new energies/vibrations which are allowing you a brand-new start at life. Watch what you wish for, because you are going to get it! Sometimes just simply letting go and knowing you are worthy will create immediate miracles/magic to happen. Don't give up. Sometimes starting with smaller changes will yield quicker responses from the Universe.

Lacking direction. This too, I've been seeing a lot of. There are many books available on career/job direction. Meditation will open up a creative channel for ideas to come to you as well. Read a lot of inspirational material, and positive affirmations.

Neutralizing Negative Karma

We touched on karma being a potential hindrance to success, let alone the evolution of one's soul, in this lifetime. Even if you're a complete skeptic, why take a chance? Why not have all bases covered? All karma is, essentially, is cause and effect; any negative vibrational influences generated by past negative thoughts and actions may be obliterated, or sublimated into God's Perfect Love energy factors. This process, like the last one, can therefore be easily integrated into your spiritual practice, eventually obtaining positive results.

The procedure for neutralizing negative karma is much the same as the previous process of re-programming one's unconscious mind in order to encourage feelings of worthiness. Take each meditative-treatment/affirmation/prayer treatment, and say it three times aloud; then, whisper it three times, finally say it mentally, three times, closing one's eyes, allowing each re-programming suggestion/affirmation to go deeper into your subconscious mind, until it takes hold. Since everything exists energetically in one's mind, any residual negative karma from this lifetime or previous lifetimes will be eventually neutralized, crucial for clearing aware unwanted mental hindrances to true growth.

Each affirmation has a category, but are all for the same purpose of neutralizing negative karma. Let's begin.

General Re-Programming/Ridding Oneself of Negative Karma

While in meditative-state, say to yourself at least three times: "I release any negative karma to God."

"I give up any negative karmic energy-factors to God."

"I release any negative karmic energy-factors that exist on any and all levels of my mind to God".

"I sublimate any negative karmic energy-factors for God's Perfect Light and Love".

"I sublimate any and all negative karmic energy-factors that may exist on all levels of my mind for God's Perfect Light and Love".

Use any one of these that resonate for you. If non feel right, substitute your own wording instead.

6 CHANGE OF CONSCIOUSNESS

In my practice, I have heard the New Age saying, "Change your Mind, Change Your Life"; if one is really accessing the Universal Mind, the result is not only a shift in attitude within the human, surface-mind, but more importantly, a shift or change of consciousness coming from the Mind of God. With this in mind, following is an excerpt from my book "Mystical Wisdom Complete".

Change of Attitude or Change of Consciousness?

Within the last decade or so, pop culture has been inundated with those "Secret" books and DVD's, along with a resurgence of the power of positive thinking philosophies. Many believe that if they maintain a positive outlook or attitude, the world will be theirs! Love, wealth, and health are the claims of those promoting "Secret" techniques, positive-thinking philosophies, and the like. All you need to do is to follow this formula or that one, and bang, all will manifest for you in all areas of your life. All of these books and DVD's have their roots in New Thought/metaphysics, and to a degree, have been proven to have a modicum of success!

This is mainly because those who have actually manifested (or materialized or shown proof, as in *The Science of Mind*) something to any degree, have succeeded in shifting their attitude to something more positive and hopeful, temporarily raising their vibration to a degree that is similar to Universal Mind's, thus creating a temporary synthesis with Universal Mind and therefore limitless potential. As I've stated before, one doesn't tell God what to do, one does what God guides them to do!

Attitude is mostly determined by exterior influences and is therefore based in the personal ego-will. Universal Consciousness is developed and nurtured from within via Contact or Mystical Meditation and Scientific-Prayer. Acquisition of things such as a new car or dress, a new job or a lover, are exterior and temporary things which often determines happiness, therefore things originating in the personal ego-will are temporary, while gratitude and appreciation, peace, and humanitarian (or Universal) love originate in the Mind of God, or Universal Mind, which is permanent. Ideas and inspiration which come from the Mind of God are permanent as well. Intuition (or God-Guidance) will often lead someone to be at the right place at the right time to follow through with actions or to meet the right person(s) which will result in ultimate (and long-lasting) prosperity and abundance.

If one can practice Mystical Meditation and Scientific-Prayer ongoing and regularly, the eventual result will be a more sharply-honed Intuition, or God-Guidance, plus overall health mind, body, and soul. One will surely be guided to their soul's purpose, or God's Will for them in this lifetime, and therefore ultimate happiness, which again, is long-lasting.

What is therefore required is a change of consciousness (for longer-lasting results) vs. a change of attitude, which results in temporary things. Higher Consciousness Meditation (also known as Contact, or Mystical Meditation) is the main tool to get one there. The more one attunes and acclimates oneself to God Conscious Awareness (peace, love, joy, happiness, Higher Intelligence, Wisdom, creativity) the greater one's chances that they will be inspired and led to receive their true riches. Merely shifting one's attitude is not enough; sure, a positive attitude will attract more positivity into your life, as opposed to if you have a negative or cynical approach, it might even attract for you a new relationship, or a better job; but these things came about as a result of superficial, temporary, and personal ego-will, and therefore will not last. This is why most, if not all, of the things one manifests as a result of the "Secret" techniques or positive thinking do not last, if they come at all. Anything that you were led to through God-Guidance/Intuition will last. Another reason is that you prayed a prayer that God guided you to pray; naturally, if you pray for what God wants for you, it will most certainly come! This is accomplished through Scientific-Prayer/Prayer Treatments combined with Mystical Meditation, which will empower the prayer. Learn more about them through my books, *Speaking Thoughts Into Existence* (ISBN-10: 1517327148 ISBN-13: 978-1517327149) and *Scientific-Prayer* (ISBN-10: 1512183717) Over time, the more you meditate, the more God's Will for you will come up to the surface, conscious level of your mind, and you will not only know what to pray for, but what to do!

Shift your consciousness, and your true, positive attitude and life will follow.

7 THE FOUR CONSIDERATIONS

Reprinted from my book, "Mystical Wisdom" is a chapter originally titled "The Four Conditions". The reason? You must take the following into consideration if you truly want to evolve your soul! Accessing the Mind of the Universe to ensure your prayers are coming from the Mind of God, plus identifying with God, (both generally and during Scientific-Prayer) and eliminating negative karma and your personal ego-identity through oneness with the Mind of the Universe will guarantee results! Read on.

The title of this chapter is a misnomer of sorts, for it suggests one of several things. It may suggest the four health conditions, or situations, of others; it may suggest other conditions which may determine something else. Although the title relates more to the latter, the apparent conditions I am about to describe are not as stringent as they may at first appear in determining one's spiritual well-being and evolution.

For our purposes herein, the main goal of meditation is for oneness with God, hence the name, Mystical or Contact Meditation. As a consequence of regular and ongoing meditation, one begins to heal one's mind, body, and soul; this happens regardless of if one is consciously aware of it, or whether one has a conscious Higher Consciousness experience or not. It naturally occurs nonetheless because as one acclimates themselves more and more to God's Perfect Love frequency during the process of becoming one (harmonizing) oneself with God during Contact Meditation, the indication of oneness is the feeling of peace and/or joy; calmness, and contentedness are also symptoms, if you will. Since everyone is spirit in human-form, it is difficult to continually feel this peace, love, harmony, joy, and contentedness; it is enough, however, to reap the rewards through regular and ongoing practice of Mystical Meditation for the healing and Intuitive development that does occur during it. If one combines the practice of Scientific-Prayer with meditation, then one's evolution advances more quickly.

During meditation, it is important as well that one conditions one's unconscious mind to also release the four conditions, as I am referring to them here. Meditative-state is the same as one of the self-hypnotic states, and therefore, re-conditioning of the unconscious mind is possible, just as re-conditioning one's mind to stop smoking or to stop over-eating is possible. The first condition, if you will, is elimination of the personal ego-will. Without this, not much else will be possible, for as long as one is ruled primarily from the human, flawed, traumatized mind, one will make decisions and take actions that are based solely on the false (not God) self; actions and thoughts will therefore be selfish, not Universal; (or humanitarian) results (if any) will be temporary, not permanent. This is a very real hindrance to the evolution of the soul, but may also be remedied. During meditation, say to yourself with a feeling of faith and determination and conviction, "I release my personal ego-will to God!" Repeat this over and over, at least three times. It's been clinically proven that any command given by another or to oneself during self-hypnotic or meditative-state will go deeper and take hold if it is said three times, over and over, over time. This is one of the most important steps towards true spiritual liberation, or evolution of the soul.

The next condition is karma.

Strictly speaking, karma is merely cause and effect; there is nothing more and nothing less to it! There is no retribution associated with it, no fear or guilt, nor religious connotations. Simply, what ever is energetically released, eventually returns, it is not just a spiritual law, it's also a law of physics! Einstein proved that whatever is released, returns in a broad circle. Nonetheless, karma is a player in ones spiritual evolution, as it can effect the process, slowing things down to have an individual heal from, and/or deal with karmic-related issues, both from previous lifetimes, as well as this current lifetime. The simple solution is to sit, while in meditative-state, and declare with conviction, "I release to God any negative karma from this and previous lifetimes!" If this feels better to you, alternatively you can declare and proclaim with conviction, "I sublimate any negative karma from previous and current lifetimes for God's Perfect Light and Love!" Whichever feels right, is the right statement for you. Again, this said at least three times, over time, will release any residual karma, and you can carry on with your life, free and clear. You must condition your unconscious mind to accept that all negative karma is released. The third condition is identifying with God. You must see yourself as pure, unconditional and Universal love. You must associate feelings of joy, contentment, peace, and harmony with yourself, since you are comprised of source! Visualize pure, white, God-Light, and see it in every cell and tissue of your body, all of the organs, bones, etc. See God's Light within you and around you, to the point that you cannot distinguish one from the other. You must be at a point where you literally smile to yourself when you think of yourself as your Higher Self, and then feel the joy and contentment that you truly are. Practice this over and over during meditation, and soon you will have conditioned yourself to identify with God, which is also a crucial step during Scientific-Prayer.

The final condition is having your prayers and thoughts come from the Mind of God, also crucial in the process of Scientific-Prayer!

This may sound at first insurmountable, after all, how does one "channel God", so-to-speak? The method, again, is simple. During meditation, state over and over again silently to yourself with faith and conviction, "My prayers and thoughts come from the Mind of God!" Stated several times in a session, and over time, your unconscious mind will accept this notion, and it will become fact. Your Intuition (God-Guidance) will be heightened and eventually honed; you will act and think purely intuitively, and you won't give it a second thought. You will recognize and follow hunches to a successful conclusion. Eliminating all fear and doubt to your connection with God, you will be acting for God, speaking for God, with great compassion and Universal Love.

If you are aware of these four conditions, and take steps to work with them, there will be little blocks to the evolution of your soul, and therefore to oneness with God.

8 ACCESSING THE MIND OF THE UNIVERSE

Originally entitled "Accessing Infinite Intelligence For True Prosperity", this was the first chapter of my book "Mystical Wisdom", but serves as review of sorts within the context of this book. Enjoy!

What is Infinite Intelligence? Is it the same as Infinite Wisdom, or Higher Intelligence? Is it the same as Cosmic Consciousness, Higher Consciousness, Higher Conscious Awareness, or First Cause? And what of Spirit? Is the word Spirit interchangeable with all of these other words? Lastly, can we use "soul" in lieu of all of the aforementioned words?

The truth of the matter is, these are all New Thought/Metaphysical/Theocentric/Mystical terms for "God". all of them interchangeable with each other, and in the context of the subject-matter contained herein, I will be using these terms liberally.

This isn't a religious book, nor is it meant to convert anyone to any particular faith; it is meant, however, to explore and analyze in depth (and from a New Thought/Metaphysical/Theocentric/Mystical) manner First Cause; a hefty goal, considering the premise (if you choose to accept that initially at all) that the only reality, all that everything is comprised of, is First Cause. By the very nature of the term "First Cause" we are led (if we allow it) to the conclusion that everything began with "First Cause".

Was there initially "nothingness" and then "somethingness", or First Cause, or was the "nothingness" comprised of First Cause? If you follow Zen Buddhism, then within the nothingness may be found the "all", or God! Hence the koan, "What is the sound of one hand clapping?" the great philosophical answer being, "no-thing". The key to achieving "oneness", "enlightenment", etc. in Zen Buddhism is meditation: the word Zen means meditation! Similarly, the key to achieving Christ Conscious Awareness, ("oneness", "enlightenment") or the point when the soul is in eternal oneness with the mind and spirit of God (in New Thought/Spiritual Mind-Science philosophies, Theocentric Psychology, Mysticism) is achieved through "Contact" or "Mystical" meditation.

The truth of the matter is, there is no sudden "lightening-bolt" or "satori" of enlightenment after a period of regular and ongoing Mystical/Contact Meditation; the experience of peace, love, joy, happiness, gratitude and appreciation is it! These are the "symptoms" of having achieved oneness at the moment with our creator/First Cause! The secret is to continually experience this joy or bliss. Some after-effects are Cosmic Consciousness, or experiencing a different "perspective" on things; some people call this having a "higher perspective", but really, it is looking at things a little differently.

In New Thought/Metaphysics/Theocentric Psychology, it is also believed that, because of a regular and ongoing contact with the energies of God, one begins to "channel" God, or become more intuitive. God's Will for us is therefore more easily accessed, and we even begin to know what to pray for, since God knows what we have need of even before we do. The chances of our prayers becoming reality therefore become greater, since we are praying God's prayer for us, and therefore it must come to pass! We are guided by God, in time, to be at the right place at the right time, and with the right people to receive our prosperity! We therefore begin to "get on track" with our "soul's purpose", also called God's Will for us in this lifetime! We know we are living our soul's purpose because we are blissfully fulfilled and happy, although our soul's purpose may change several times throughout our lifetime, as we grow and evolve!

This living of our soul's purpose, and the subsequent joy, peace, and happiness is referred-to as true prosperity.

Prosperity is therefore achieved through the ongoing and regular practice of Mystical Meditation for the purposes of contact with Higher Consciousness, and therefore peace, love, and joy.

9 THE UNIVERSAL MIND AND YOUR HEALTH

Originally titled "Mystical Wisdom and Your Health" from my book "Mystical Wisdom", I feel it crucial to reiterate some previous points about how one accesses the Universal Mind for health and wholeness.

If "God", or "Infinite Intelligence" is accessed through the ongoing and regular practice of Contact or Mystical Meditation, and the experience manifests as peace, love, and joy, how can this also result in a healthy mind, body, and soul?

If you buy the premise that our bodies become attuned to the Perfect frequencies and energies of God through frequent and regular contact with God via Mystical Meditation, then it follows that every cell and tissue of our body, mind, and soul will also resonate to that Perfect frequency which is God. How can the mind, body, and soul not be healed of any supposed illnesses while resonating to God's Perfect Love?

A further concept which will begin to help in this assimilation of information is that of us being holistically inclined, that is, we are "Psycho-Physical Units". We cannot have a single thought (conscious or subconscious) without it affecting our mind (emotions) and impacting our soul; we also cannot help but have our emotions (mind) and our soul be influenced by our body; as well, our soul impacts (positively or negatively) our mind and our body. Consider these examples: suppose we are angry or moody; our posture often reflects this as we trudge along in our day, and we become more and more sad throughout the day unless something comes along to change this. Another example is this: if we are in physical discomfort, (back pain for example) then our mood and posture will be affected! Therefore we are Psycho-Physical Units: our mind affects our body and soul, our soul affects our mind and our body, and our body affects our mind and our soul. We are holistically constructed.

How do we stop this vicious cycle? The answer, quite simply, is that we do not! This is the very nature of how we were made, and therefore it's perfect the way it is. What we can do to work with what God gave us, is to regularly and ongoingly practice Contact (Mystical) Meditation as the resulting attuning of our bodies to God's Perfection will eventually affect us in positive ways. This is not to say that we must not also follow our physician's advice, and take any medication he prescribes; we must also exercise regularly for mind, body, and soul as well. The combination of eating natural and whole-foods, physician's advice, as well as exercise and meditation will strike the perfect balance for our health mind, body, and soul.

Another ingredient to be added to your health regiment that must be mentioned at this point is prayer. I'm not referring to the traditional religious, or pleading prayer, but to a more self-empowering type of prayer sometimes called Prayer Treatments, or Affirmative or Scientific-Prayer. I've written some books outlining in detail the methodology, (*Speaking Thoughts Into Existence*, ISBN-10: 1517327148 ISBN-13: 978-1517327149 and *Scientific Prayer*, ISBN-10: 1512183717) and I'd like to touch on it here, as you will find the combination of Mystical Meditation together with Prayer Treatments or Scientific-Prayer to be a powerful contributor to your health mind, body, and soul.

Very generally, Prayer Treatments or Scientific-Prayer (so-called because of its specific steps which have been clinically-proven) may also be called Affirmative-Prayer, and even Meditational Treatments, not to be confused with the popular use of affirmations for manifesting your heart's desires. What your personal ego-will desires and therefore may manifest will only be temporary; only what Higher Intelligence may bring into your conscious, surface mind will likely come to pass as a result of Scientific-Prayer. Nonetheless, while meditating, (practicing Mystical Meditation) the steps are Unifying and Identifying, (with God) Denying, (whatever the unwanted situation is, be it ill-health, poverty, loneliness) Affirming and Declaring with strong emotions and faith and belief that it has already happened, (what you desire, be it better health, finances, or earthly love) Releasing and Letting It Be So, (for the Universe to help it transpire and therefore not holding on to it) finally stamping with strong conviction the conclusion "And So It Is!" Note that faith, belief, and conviction are key and crucial ingredients to this type of prayer; if you lack any of this, you must develop faith, belief, and conviction in yourself and your future, otherwise the results will take longer to come to pass. Note as well that to prayer successfully, the idea for the prayer must come from your intuition, a.k.a.

the Mind of God. Ongoing and regular meditation will eventually result in you being a conduit for God's Will/Intuition. The time-frame varies with every individual.

Combining the advice of your physician, healthy diet and exercise, combined with your spiritual practice of Contact/Mystical Meditation with Scientific/Affirmative Prayer will without question contribute to a healthy mind, body, and soul.

10 IN SUMMATION

It can be agreed at this point that the Universal Mind is the Highest Intelligence of the universe, the sum total of the complete knowledge and wisdom of the ages.

It contains the key to all of your plans, past, present, and future, and if you adhere to the New Thought/metaphysical principle that everything is already successful in the Mind of the Universe/Mind of God, then we all have much to look forward (or backward) to. All we need do is to get out of our own way/the Mind of God and allow It to manifest/express Itself! We may do this by casting aside our temporary ego-identity and allow for a more permanent God Mind to take us over, consciously and other wise, to guide us Intuitively towards a happier, more prosperous life.

Add to this an identification with the Universal Mind/Mind of God, along with casting aside/giving up to God any negative karmic thought-forms in our unconscious mind potentially adversely affecting any outcome, and we can't help but begin to think and to pray from this great, infinite field of love, joy, and wisdom known as the Universal Mind..

Imagine allowing oneself to create from the Mind of the Universe: to allow any works of art, music, and literature formed in the Mind of God to begin to take on physical embodiment through ourselves and the vessel known as our physical existence…how utterly and infinitely beautiful would that be? Yes, we hold the key to this allowing, to stepping aside and having infinite beauty and wisdom to form and shape through Higher Consciousness/Contact or Mystical Meditation!

The simple, yet powerful and crucial act of self-care that is meditation will enhance our thoughts and prayers; more importantly, it begins to allow for a "mind-shaft" if you will, for God's wisdom to rise up from the center and nucleus of our mind to the conscious or surface levels. The healing energies of the Mind of God begins to seep up, and our body begins to respond emotionally to these frequencies; reaching all levels of our mind, healing them, and thus allowing for a higher quality of life mind, body, and soul, since we are all Psycho-Physical Units, or holistic in nature.

More than this, our Intuition (or God-Guidance) becomes more finely tuned as it responds more and more to the Wisdom of the Universal Mind. You will trust more and more what that "still small voice" tells you. You'll become more optimistic, a "Pollyanna" if-you-will, among cynics, but that won't discourage you, for deep down, (or maybe not so deep down) you will recognize yourself and others for Who and What they truly Are: living, breathing manifestations of the stars and of the heavens, having taken image, shape, form, and embodiment! As your vibration and the energy-factors of your body begin to take on the same Higher resonance as the Mind of God through meditation, you'll find that whatever prayers were formed first in the Mind of God become manifest through yourself and your God-Guided actions! If the Mind of the Universe has willed it that you have a certain lifestyle, (because of your Soul's Purpose/God's Will for you in this lifetime) you are then guided to achieve it, whatever it is! For some it may appear as luxury, to others it may appear as humble and understated, but you yourself know that whatever it may be, you are happy and content knowing where it originated from. Your use of Scientific/Affirmative-Prayer along with Prayer Treatments begin to heal yourself and others, since there is only one Life in the Universe; your optimism about your life and others become manifest in the proof of health, wholeness, and completeness within yourself and others! You can truly witness the Mind of the Universe in action in the prosperity and abundance within and around yourself.

Perhaps there is something, after all, to all this talk about God and the Mind of the Universe.

CONCLUSION

I'd like to mention at this point something obvious; please do not be taken in by some pie-in-the-sky offerings of some "secret" magical manifestation formula. The following is from my book *Speaking thoughts Into Existence*,(ISBN-10: 1517327148 and ISBN-13: 978-1517327149) and is from the chapter called *Pitfalls to Manifesting*.

Manifesting isn't all money, love, houses, and cars. To do a demonstration/materialization/manifestation FIRST of the *healing* kind is what is most desired. In fact, as already stated, this was the original intention of Scientific Prayer/Affirmative/Meditative Mind-Treatments. Work first towards proclaiming with faith, belief, and determination that a person is healed of a particular ailment or dis-ease, and then have it happen. If that's not happening, you're not doing it right, either you don't have enough faith, or you don't feel worthy yourself of perfect health, you haven't cleaned up enough Karma, and/or you haven't connected with your Highest Self, becoming One with the Infinite Mind. Try, try again. I guarantee you that if you first try to manifest things to benefit yourself and you actually succeed, unless that was meant to be, or that the idea came from the Mind of God, then it will eventually disappear, or you will lose it. I know because that all happened to me.

Another Story Or Two

When I was working at Reflections Books in Coquitlam, Canada as a psychic reader ten or so years ago, I got all caught up in "The Secret", which a co-worker turned me on to. "What is this *Secret*", I thought to myself, "that everyone is talking about?" Turns out it had to do with The

Law of Attraction, a very real metaphysical law (as previously outlined) but I have to admit at the time, it sounded airy-fairy "New-Age-y" to me. "Harmless enough", I thought, "let's give it a go!" So I borrowed a boot-leg copy of "The Secret" from Grace to watch, to determine whether or not I wanted to actually buy a real copy. Let me tell you, it completely changed my life that evening! The relatively high production values, cinematography, and interviews with people with "D.D." after their name, as well as "Dr." preceding their names seemed to add credibility to the whole thing. Although it had an air of romanticism to it, it also had the ability to lift me up, to take me to a place I haven't been to in years; I didn't realize this was part of the process, lifting one's vibration so high, one becomes One with God, therefore whatever is in one's mind, becomes real! This is an example of The Law of Correspondence or Equivalents, together with The Law of Magnetic Attraction and The Law of Cause and Effect duplicating what is coming from the Mind of God. Powerful stuff; way more powerful than I realized at the time, again, I didn't know that I was dealing with spiritual Laws that are real. What an amazing introduction to New Thought and metaphysics "The Secret" is, and which took me on the path to eventually earning my Bachelors, Masters, and three Doctorates! However, I didn't realize at the time that I was like a child playing with a loaded gun!

In short order, I manifested new leather couches, and even a brand-new car! Readings kept coming to me in abundance, so I was never short on cash. One day, I did find myself needing to put an extra $20. in the bank to cover a payment. I was to get paid the following week and needed the cash right now. This is how that $20. manifested: I realized that I had misplaced my car-keys to my new Jeep, yes, I succeeded in manifesting a second vehicle by-the-way! I looked and looked around the house to no avail. I even pulled up the cushions of those new/secondhand leather couches, and voila, a wallet! Feverishly I opened the wallet to find the I.D. of a Japanese exchange student from years ago, long-gone I was sure. But in this wallet as well was Japanese Yen, foreign currency of which I had no idea of the value. Something inside me said to run across the street to my bank, and ask about this money. It turned out to be equal in value to the $20. I needed, exactly! No more, no less! The Universe was again working its magic! I immediately deposited it, thus covering the amount. My car keys? Conveniently sitting on top of a compartment between my Jeep's seat and the door, the Universe causing this search so that I'd find the $20. I was floored again, riding high this wave of abundance and manifestation which I attributed to "The Secret" and The Law of Attraction! Several clients healed themselves of mental strain and poverty as a result of my passion about "The Secret" which I led them to buy. Issues of love were again solved by my leading clients to "The Secret".

My enthusiasm would soon wane for this miracle of prosperity and abundance, this doorway to success and happiness.

Without too much thinking, I kept on manifesting, for some reason wanting to trade in my beloved Jeep for something bigger and flashier, a luxurious Dodge Ram turbo-charged truck! This flashy red monster set me back my Jeep which I had to turn in, and $800. a month payments on top of the third car which I manifested for my wife and all of those monthly payments. I was starting to feel pressure that I had not felt in years, since the days of my first bankruptcy, whose energy still felt familiar to me. I believe it was this remembering of "poverty-energy" in my mind that began to co-create it for real, as opposed to my newly remembered abundance/prosperity energy. It's not that one is stronger than the other, merely present! In short time, I went form prosperity and abundance to bankruptcy again, all caused because I didn't stop to take a breath and meditate! Had I not rushed into those payments frantically, but asked for a day to think about it and breath and meditate, I'm sure I would have avoided all of that financial trouble. Nonetheless, like the story of the lost keys, this bankruptcy resulted in us clearing away all debts, thereby living debt-free! Burdon-less, we continue to thrive, living within our means and not owing a cent. We got to keep one car and did successfully pay it off.

This is just one example of mis-using a mindless spiritual principle. It wasn't Karma, it wasn't retribution, merely not thinking/using common God-given sense, and meditating to avoid trouble. This is the thing; "The Secret", The Law of Attraction and all the other spiritual Laws cannot teach you to be smart; it won't encourage you to use your Intuition; it won't help you to avoid life; it is not some magic-wand that will suddenly make everything right. In the words of Spider Man, "With great power comes great responsibility", and I was shirking my duty of responsibility, and solemnly honoring these great gifts from the Universe, these great spiritual principles. No more, no less. In the wise words of Thomas Tusser, "A fool and his money are soon parted."

It is also important to add at this point that every soul in this lifetime is not the same; some are "baby-souls", and other ones are "intermediate-souls". Very few (if any) are "advanced souls", otherwise they might not have chosen to reincarnate again, although every advanced soul has the choice to do that or not, usually to teach unconditional love/Universal Love and compassion to the world. The Christ-Mind that was in Jesus, the Buddha, and other profits who walked the earth (including Mother Teresa) were all advanced souls. Thus, God has given us so many religions and faiths, to suit the particular soul-group whether they are "baby" or "intermediate". The same applies to the concept of spiritual laws, which were created within the Mind of the Universe so that baby and intermediate souls could at least begin to understand how this great Primal Light Energy/First Cause/Mind of God works. So don't worry if one belief-system which worked for you no longer does, or one spiritual system/philosophy that never resonated for you suddenly does; one must "go with the flow" and adapt as best we can in this lifetime, and with the help of the Mind of God/Universal Mind, how can we go far wrong?

Enjoy this ongoing journey; I'm pleased and honored to be a little part of it.

Peace and Richest Blessings,

Rev. Dr. Michael H. Likey, D.D. Ph.D. PsyThD. H.Dip.

ABOUT THE AUTHOR

Dr. Michael Likey is an International Author, Clinical Hypnotherapist, Doctor of Theocentric Psychology, Producer/Host of his BlogTalk Radio show, Live-Streamed Video-Broadcasts, and creator of his Transcendence System. He has an H.Dip. (*Diploma of Clinical Hypnotherapy*) from The Robert Shields College of Hypnotherapy, England. Michael is also certified through Robert Shields as a *Fear Elimination Therapist*, (2004) and is also a triple-Doctoral graduate: a D.D., *Doctor of Divinity Specializing in Spiritual Healing*, from the University of Metaphysics, a Ph.D. *Specializing in Mystical Research* from the University of Sedona, and a PsyTh.D., *Doctor of Theocentric Psychology*, from the University of Sedona, Dr. Masters, CEO. Both the University of Metaphysics, and the University of Sedona, as well as it's parent organization, The International Metaphysical Ministry, were founded by Dr. Masters, CEO. Dr. Michael is the author of the popular and globally-available books **"Spiritual Mind-Science And Your Soul"**, **"The Science of the Soul"**, **"Magic Happens!"**, **"Journey of the Mind, Journey of the Soul"**, **"The Spiritual Laws Of The Universe"**, **"Scientific Prayer"**, and **"Dr. Likey's Transcendence System"** in addition to a **dozen e-books** (available on the Amazon Kindle Store), and is also Founder/CEO/Spiritual-Director of his own spiritual gatherings/programs.
He is a Member of the **International Metaphysical Ministry**.
Contact: dr.likey@gmail.com
Facebook: https://www.facebook.com/Dr.MichaelLikey
Twitter: https://twitter.com/MichaelLikey
YouTube: https://www.youtube.com/user/SoulScienceTV
Website: http://www.drmichaellikey.com

Other Works by Dr. Michael Likey

Books

- **Mystical Wisdom Complete**-ISBN-10: 1543020305

- **Mystical Self-Hypnosis**-ISBN-10: 1542755301

- **Real Problems, Real Solutions**-ISBN-10: 1540447588

- **Mystical Wisdom**-ISBN-10: 1535347775

- **Working Through Trauma Spiritually**-ISBN-10: 1537443100

- **The Mind-The Key to Spiritual Healing**-ISBN-10: 1537319566

- **Dr. Michael's The Key to the Soul**-ISBN-10: 1532946929

- **Dr. Michael's Complete Soul Oracle Cards Manual**-ISBN-10: 1530829623

- **The Complete Spiritual Laws of the Universe**-ISBN-10: 1530735173

- **Speaking Thoughts Into Existence**-ISBN-10: 1517327148

- **Master Reiki**-ISBN-10: 1515026248

- **Dr. Likey's Transcendence System**-ISBN-10: 1514755289

- **Spiritual Mind-Science and Your Soul**-ISBN-10: 1514275104

- **Scientific Prayer**-ISBN-10: 1512183717

- **Journey of the Mind, Journey of the Soul**-ISBN-10: 1440131074

- **The Science of the Soul**-ISBN-10: 1462061885

- **Magic Happens!**-ISBN-10: 059569473X

DVD's
- **Master Reiki-**ASIN: B0131SHL7M
CD's
- **Dr. Michael's Meditational Treatments**-ASIN: B015GINO0I

Reviews

"I just finished reading your book and I absolutely loved it! I was so inspired and motivated while reading it. Your book is so wonderful and I want you to teach me the tools from your book. I've never emailed anyone after I read their book and I really hope you will reply to this email.
Again thank you for sharing your knowledge and wisdom and I am so thankful I came upon your book in a bookstore."
-Rebecca-

"I have known Rev. Dr. Michael for at least ten years, and I've been grateful to call him both a peer and a friend. In his persistent efforts to help others, he has taken it upon himself to constantly do research (both personal and professional), and to this end he has earned numerous credentials and degrees in his related fields. I have rarely seen him say "no" to assist others, and his professional skills, God-given talents, as well as his consistence to be all he can be has also resulted in him writing several books which I have the privilege of owning.
Dr. Michael shares these ancient and time-proven tools that you'll find are infinitely worth practicing, revisiting, and living for yourself".
-Grace Talson,
www.movingforwardwithgrace.com

"Dr. Likey is an accomplished metaphysician with decades of experience, and in this, his latest book, he shares insights based on his lengthy pastoral and hypnotherapeutic career. This book is a worthy development of that study combining metaphysics with an easy to adopt frame for a better life. I know few people more widely versed in metaphysical study, and it shows in the astonishing variety of influences at play – enjoy!"
-Adam S. Adams, CPC MH CISH CHt.

"Dr. Likey challenges and encourages new methods of self-exploration and discovery through new and ancient wisdom. His unique take on classic and modern therapy and techniques leaves the reader with a greater understanding of mind and soul. His information is both practical and simple to implement into your life. Dr. Likey's personal writing style makes for an easy and interesting read".
-**Sara Adams**, Owner, Finding Avalon - Spiritual ReConnection through Avalonian Archetypes
www.finding-avalon.com

"You've...helped me transcend much of the fear I was living with when I first started coming to the gatherings on Sunday mornings-I feel quite fearless now...you've helped reinforce the value of life/living for me through your tireless work. Thank you again."
-**S.K.**

"Rev. Dr. Michael is the amazing host of Dr. Michael's Soul Dialogue radio show. I had the privilege of being a guest on his show and was touched by his insight into the history of spirituality, relationships' dynamics as well as his deep knowledge of the human soul. I truly believe that Dr. Michael is providing a great show that can help people in their personal growth and spiritual search."
-**Milena Cerin**

Top Qualities: Personable, Expert, High Integrity
"Dr. Likey brings a mixture of new thought, traditional psychology and parapsychology to his client sessions. He approaches his work with consideration to all aspects of the clients situation and goes the extra mile to ensure his council is complete and comprehensive. I recommend Dr. Likey's services in combination with alternative healing (e.g. acupuncture, naturopathic, light therapy), and traditional mental/emotional therapy, as well as for lighter "am I on the right track" counsel."
-**L. Miller**

Top Qualities: Great Results, Personable, Good Value
"I have attended a number of Michael's meditation evenings where I had a great number of experiences being guided through my spiritual development. I found Michael to be very intuitive, patient and perceptive of his clients needs. I have also worked with Michael doing healing work and I learned quite a bit from his extensive knowledge and practical skills."
-M. Chong

Top Qualities: Great Results, Expert, High Integrity
"Dr. Likey's abilities in the metaphysical field are unmatched in my opinion, his ability to provide insight into your life will amaze you. Dr. Likey provides many other services to enhance your life, seminars, Reiki therapy, and many books related to living a better life.
I highly recommended visiting Dr. Likey."
-T. Hobbs

Top Qualities: Great Results, Personable, Expert
"I was privileged to study Reiki under Mike's expert care, and was astounded by the depth of knowledge that he has on all matters metaphysical.
 The ability to turn the arcane into the comprehensible and digestible is rare, yet Mike has it in spades.
 His personal qualities are outstanding, and the whole experience of learning from him was enjoyable and deeply rewarding.

"Michael is a great teacher - knows his stuff, he takes research and experience and blends them seamlessly into practical and fun trainings."
-S. Adams MH, CHt

"You are truly a Master and have shown this over and over... God bless and reward you".
-Patti

Made in the USA
Columbia, SC
01 January 2023